WHITEHEAD AND BRADLEY

SUNY Series in Systematic Philosophy
Robert Cummings Neville

FRANCIS HERBERT BRADLEY   ALFRED NORTH WHITEHEAD

WHITEHEAD AND BRADLEY

A Comparative Analysis

LEEMON B. MC HENRY

State University
of New York
Press

Published by
State University of New York Press, Albany

© 1992 State University of New York

For information, address State University of New York
Press, State University Plaza, Albany, N.Y. 12246

Library of Congress Cataloging-in-Publication Data

McHenry, Leemon B., 1956–
    Whitehead and Bradley : a comparative analysis / Leemon B.
McHenry.
        p.   cm.
    Includes bibliographical references and index.
    ISBN 0-7914-0915-5 (alk. paper) : $44.50. — ISBN 0-7914-0916-3
(pbk. : alk. paper) : $14.95
    1. Whitehead, Alfred North, 1861–1947.   2. Bradley, F. H. (Francis
Herbert), 1846–1924.   3. Metaphysics—History—20th century
I. Title.
B1674.W354M34   1992   91-12725
192—dc20   CIP

To Joyce and Leemon

CONTENTS

PREFACE AND ACKNOWLEDGMENTS

The present study attempts to examine the affinities and contrasts in the metaphysical systems of A. N. Whitehead and F. H. Bradley. As a comparative analysis, however, the study does not attempt to give equal attention to every aspect of both thinkers; rather, its primary concern is the influence of Bradley on Whitehead and the problems that bind them together under the genre of philosophical idealism. But aside from this historical concern, the book also attempts to work out solutions to metaphysical problems, especially those that occur where process philosophy and absolute idealism conflict. I generally defend Whitehead's view where conflict does arise, but I am not a follower of the Whiteheadian school that has formed in praise of his thought. Nevertheless, unlike the vast majority of analytic philosophers working in the field today, I do not think that total neglect is the proper approach to appreciating his genius. In my view, Whitehead and Bradley rank among the greatest thinkers in the Western tradition alongside of Descartes, Kant, Hume, Leibniz, Spinoza, and Hegel.

This work was written in two stages. The most substantial portions were worked out in Edinburgh, Scotland, at the University of Edinburgh—the city and university in which Whitehead himself delivered his Gifford Lectures and which, on an earlier occasion, he referred to as "the capital of British metaphysics, haunted by the shade of Hume." It is no small debt that I owe the Faculty of Arts at the University of Edinburgh for generous support during this time. The second stage of radical revision and restructuring was undertaken in the odd moments stolen from teaching at Davidson College, Central Michigan University, and Wittenberg University. A Faculty Research Grant from Davidson College allowed me to return to Edinburgh and regain my enthusiasm for completing the book.

Various parts of previously published work are incorporated into this book. Parts of chapters 2, 3, and 5 were published as "Time, Relations and Dependence" in *The Southern Journal of Philosophy*, 1983. A small section of chapter 1 is taken from "The Axiomatic Matrix of Whitehead's *Process and Reality*," which appeared in *Process Studies* in 1986. And an earlier version of chapter 4 appears as "Bradley, James and Whitehead on Relations," published in the *Journal of Speculative Philosophy* in 1989. I wish to thank the editors of these journals for permission to republish these articles here.

The 1920 photograph of Whitehead is reproduced here courtesy of Mrs. T. North Whitehead. The portrait of Bradley is by R. Grenville Eves, and is reproduced here by permission of the Warden and Fellows of Merton College, Oxford.

My single most important obligation is to Timothy Sprigge for his invaluable criticism of this work in its early stages, which is not to say that he would be entirely satisfied with the result. Much of our discussion of the philosophical issues herein occurred during frequent walks between the David Hume Tower and Edinburgh's West End, many amid gale winds blowing off the Firth of Forth.

I owe thanks to two students of Whitehead, Dorothy Emmet and the late Victor Lowe. Charles Hartshorne must also be mentioned for faithful correspondence during the Edinburgh days. And in the final review process, I benefited from several critical evaluations provided by the press. The author of one of these is known to me: George R. Lucas, Jr.

My thanks are also due to Jim McKenna for his acute eye in copyediting the manuscript.

Over the last ten years my views have been undeniably shaped by a philosophic milieu that has included Ronald Burr, Paul Sharkey, Forrest Wood, Errol Bedford, Stanley Eveling, Lewis Ford, William Brenner, Alfred Mele, John Heil, Irwin Goldstein, Gary Fuller, Fred Adams, Don Reed, Bob Levy and Vis Klive. I wish here to express my gratitude to the above-mentioned for providing the context for various types of philosophic sparring as well as the opportunity to keep abreast with contemporary philosophy.

Renée, as always, has been most understanding and supportive during my preoccupation with this work. Finally, this book is dedicated to my parents. I have enjoyed their unfailing support during the years that this work has been under way.

CHAPTER 1

Introduction

THE CENTRAL PLAN OF THIS ESSAY

Alfred North Whitehead is widely recognized as having made profound contributions to the shape of thought in the twentieth century. As a professional mathematician trained at Cambridge, his work with Bertrand Russell, *Principia Mathematica*, gained him a prominent place in the history of logic. His work in the philosophy of physics, particularly his critical evaluation of Einstein and his attempt to advance his own form of relativity theory, made him a central figure in the debate over the emerging scientific hypotheses in the 1920s. And, once he emigrated to America and flourished as a professional philosopher at Harvard, the fruits of many years of philosophic contemplation resulted in a system of metaphysics that radically altered our ordinary thinking about ourselves and our world. His views on science, religion, education, history, and civilization have captured the imagination and inspired numerous thinkers in their own specialized areas of learning. But for all this, Whitehead remains an enigma for most philosophers today and his work has little impact on the mainstream of philosophical thought in the English-speaking world.

By Whitehead's own understanding of the evolution of philosophic trends, historical epochs immerse themselves in speculative construction and are then pruned back by periods of intense analytic rigor and adherence to method. But once the methodologies exhaust themselves and the discussion of the central problems becomes fatigued, speculation again becomes crucial to novelty and the advance of knowledge.[1] During the period in which Whitehead himself produced his metaphysics, speculative construction was flourishing in physics, but otiose in philosophy. The developments in logical positivism and linguistic analysis set the stage for orthodoxy in this century, and Whitehead's thought was left for a handful of his students or for those unswayed by the dominant trends. Today, however, the situation is much more

1

open to the problems Whitehead attempted to solve and to the subject of metaphysics generally, but still very few thinkers are prepared or willing to master his system. This situation is especially unfortunate since his philosophy offers profound insight into a number of contemporary problems in ontology, epistemology, personal identity, and the philosophy of science. But in what follows it is not my purpose to defend Whitehead's general conception of philosophy against contemporary modes of analysis. Rather I take the endeavor of the speculative philosopher to be an essential undertaking and concentrate my attention on one major influence on Whitehead, namely, nineteenth-century Oxford philosopher, Francis Herbert Bradley.

Although Whitehead is generally regarded as a realist, especially when viewed for his concerns to construct a foundation for twentieth-century physics, the metaphysics put forth in *Process and Reality* cannot be classified strictly as realist in orientation. On many epistemological issues, he retains his loyalty to the line of thought that reacted against neo-Hegelianism, but at the same time, Whitehead's adherence to the idea that experience is the fundamental basis of reality puts him squarely within the idealist tradition. It is in this connection that his relation to Bradley provides an insight into what Whitehead himself thought of his final results. In one of his essays he writes, "I admit a very close affiliation with Bradley . . . " as he explains his affinities and contrasts to idealism.[2] And again in the preface to *Process and Reality*, Whitehead describes the final outcome of his cosmology as "not so greatly different" from Bradley's position.[3] Although he is greatly indebted to Bradley's concept of 'feeling' as an "implicit repudiation of the doctrine of 'vacuous actuality'" his disagreements focus primarily on various problems of accepting the Absolute as the final transcendent Reality. He frequently referred to this position as the "block universe" devoid of process. This is what he means when he says that: "if this cosmology be deemed successful, it becomes natural at this point to ask whether the type of thought involved be not a transformation of some main doctrines of Absolute Idealism onto a realistic basis."[4] Whitehead turned the Absolute upside down by deriving the solidarity of the universe from the actuality in each individual occasion of experience. For him, nature grows in a synthetic, creative manner from bottom up.

Whether or not Whitehead is successful in his transformation of absolute idealism largely depends on his interpretation of the nature and function of relations in experience. Hence, in what follows, it is necessary to examine Bradley's arguments against metaphysical pluralism. Although the concept of 'feeling' is a crucial point of departure for both philosophers, Bradley was quite insistent that the very essence of feeling is nondiscrete and nonrelational. Bradley therefore argued that relations are self-contradictory and cannot accurately characterize the nature of ultimate Reality. The strength of this conclusion leads him to the view that a genuine plurality of individuals is impossible and that reality must be a nonrelational One. Whitehead, on the other hand, takes relatedness to be an essential defining characteristic of his occasions of experience; each must enter into relationship as an ingredient of process. This is the fundamental issue of disagreement between Whitehead and Bradley, and in many respects it is the main focus of the present essay. For Bradley the connectedness of Reality cannot be accurately characterized by the relational form of thought, whereas Whitehead contends that nature, divided at its natural joints, proves relational.

The fact that Whitehead was a successor to Bradley and in large measure accepts his theory of 'feeling' provides a certain strategy for the present work. What I offer is an analysis and evaluation of the different consequences drawn from the interpretation of 'feeling', and in so doing I attempt to answer how "the final outcome is after all not so greatly different."

IDEALISM AND REALISM

Idealism as used throughout our philosophical heritage has been attached to numerous and conflicting sources. Though all varieties acknowledge mind as ultimately real, the issues that divide one type of idealism from another could occupy the better part of this introduction. A cursory survey might include: Platonic idealism, panpsychistic idealism, subjective idealism, transcendental idealism and absolute idealism, all of which differ from one another drastically and assert very different principles about the nature of reality. Taken in the most general sense, however, idealism opposes any form of materialism that asserts the insentient, purposeless reality of matter. In this regard Whitehead and Bradley unite in attacking the materialist-mechanistic worldview of a universe composed of what Whitehead calls "vacuous actualities." Sentient experience is therefore fundamental to both Whitehead and Bradley. Experience, or the more specific term, 'feeling', as the basis of reality, provides the point of contact whereby both philosophers align themselves with the idealist tradition.

One difficulty arises that may blur the distinction between absolute idealism and Platonic idealism. That is, in Plato's philosophy, the temporal process is often construed as "appearances" of the fundamental reality of the permanent Forms. This view can be confused with Bradley's distinction between appearance and Reality and with the notion that finite experience transcends its immediacy as it becomes transmuted within the experience of the Absolute. The crucial difference, however, is that Bradley does not espouse a complete disjunction between appearance and reality as Plato is usually thought to do in his middle dialogues. Whitehead seems to mistake Bradley's view when he takes appearance to mean illusory rather than merely finite.[5] As Bradley put the point, appearance, though incomplete in itself, is "the stuff of which the Universe is made."[6] Finite appearances might be better characterized as "relatively unreal" instead of illusory since they are mere abstractions of an infinite totality.

Whitehead's insistence on the reality of temporal process was a central concern throughout his philosophical career. He repudiated the view that the supreme reality is a perfection of changeless order. This notion has been dominant in the Platonic and Christian traditions where transience and change are subordinate to the essentially static conception of eternity. It is here that we find the notion of mere appearance, and, unfortunately, Bradley is often mistaken as holding this view. Bradley's Absolute is a timeless perfection unifying the diversity of experience. However, the diverse elements essentially qualify the Absolute in some degree and cannot be taken as illusory.

What is not possible, in Bradley's view, is the genuine individuality of the various appearances. It is on this score that Whitehead parts company with Bradley. The setting of the metaphysical problem, for Whitehead, is both realistic and pluralistic. Each actuality exists in its own right. The notion of a common world, including ourselves and other actualities, is then transformed from strict realism to idealism by the manner in which each individual is temporally connected to form a coherent universe of experience.

WHITEHEAD'S PROCESS REALISM AND PHILOSOPHICAL METHOD

As mentioned above, the basis for Whitehead's realism was closely tied to his concern to construct a cosmology that would accommodate the advances in twentieth-century physics and biology. The beginning of this century was clearly a time of reorganization, and Whitehead recognized that the fall of the seventeenth-century cosmology would require a new comprehensive system that would bring together the fundamental advances under a single unifying concept. In *Process and Reality*, Whitehead achieved the most detailed exposition of this cosmological system, and much of it embodies his earlier interests in the philosophical foundations of natural science. Though the metaphysics contained therein should not be considered a mere continuation of the problems he faced in the philosophy of natural science, the earlier investigations certainly pave the way for the speculative synthesis.

The emphasis on the new realism that dominated philosophical thought at the outset of this century was clearly a result of the discrepancy between the larger conception of idealist systems and the important results that the special sciences accumulated. The nature/spirit dichotomy that was previously reconciled within a Hegelian framework now proved too much slanted in favor of spirit and was of little help in understanding the complexities of evolution, electromagnetic theory, or relativity physics. Since many of the realists believed that idealism was grandiose and actually thwarted the advance of knowledge, they sought to shed any remnant of a philosophy that was regarded as an antiquated relic of the Victorian age. Russell, Moore, Alexander, Broad, and Nunn were the dominant figures in Britain who reacted against idealism as an inadequate foundation for the sciences. And Whitehead is also justifiably linked with this wave of thought, especially in his premetaphysical period.[7] However, there is very little in Whitehead's philosophy that he shares with the Russell-Moore line of thought. At no point throughout his philosophy of natural science or his metaphysics did he hold an exclusive doctrine of external relations where entities are believed to exist in complete independence of one another. As early as *The Principles of Natural Knowledge*, his view of nature is essentially holistic, but, unlike Bradley's holism, Whitehead's conception of nature is diversified into overlapping, four-dimensional events structured by various complexities of objects. The fact that he was in a position to take account of the major advances in science gave him a basis very different from Bradley's on which to construct his system of natural knowledge, and finally, his cosmology.

What does justify Whitehead's association with the realists is an epistemological issue concerning the relation between mind and nature—what is perceived is not just one's own mental states but a direct apprehension of nature, and this is quite real. The most important consequence of this epistemological realism is that the datum for natural science is not at all mental. Scientific investigation requires that its objects be separate and prior to perception and thought. Whitehead thus argues against the subjective idealist that no assertions concerning nature can be verified if what is perceived is only a fact of individual psychology.[8] This doctrine plays an important role throughout Whitehead's work, namely for the sake of securing the basis of scientific objectivity. In *The Concept of Nature*, Whitehead's doctrine that "nature is closed to mind" served the purpose of limiting his inquiry to that which appears to us in sense perception, but this idea did not imply a metaphysical disjunction between nature and mind, for the doctrine as to how mind functions in nature was left to his later work.[9]

Once process is accepted as the fundamental notion in Whitehead's metaphysics, the extensive properties of nature become dependent upon one ontological type that is characterized by the becoming of experience. His thought radiates as he moves from the attempt to provide a philosophy of natural science to a comprehensive metaphysics. Where in his earlier work his aim is to provide a unifying concept for the reorganization of theoretical physics, the ideal of the later work is an all-inclusive theory "which will set in assigned relationships within itself all that there is for knowledge, for feeling, and for emotion."[10] The result is a general hypothesis concerning the nature of ultimate reality, and not just the nature of the physical world.

In the philosophy of natural science, Whitehead says we are thinking "homogeneously" about nature when we are limiting our concerns by confining attention to the natural sciences.[11] We are here "concerned only with Nature, that is, with the object of perceptual knowledge, and not with the synthesis of the knower and known."[12] However, once we are thinking "heterogeneously" about nature so as to include mind, the spectrum widens as does the range of application. Insofar as we include the nature of mind in our pursuit, he argues that "it must be one of the motives of a complete cosmology to construct a system of ideas which brings the aesthetic, moral, and religious interests into relation with those concepts of the world which have their origin in natural science."[13] Here the emphasis is placed on systematic construction, and metaphysical inquiry is pursued with an eye for interconnections between the different departments of knowledge. As he said in one of his few surviving letters, his task was "to evolve one way of speaking which applies equally to physics, physiology, and to our aesthetic experiences."[14] His philosophy of organism begins with the perceiver and his immediate environment. Once generalized to the metaphysical level, this notion becomes the basis for understanding relations between all actualities.

Whitehead saw that while many thinkers accepted the advances of the twentieth-century revolution in physics, they still held an implicit conception of matter from the seventeenth-century cosmology. In this sense the transition from the concept of inert matter to the concept of energetic vibrations was not complete. While many were content to think of energy in conventional materialistic or positivistic terms, Whitehead argued that this was simply an inability to move forward in accordance with scientific advance. Progress in knowledge demands that science will not "be combining various propositions which tacitly presuppose inconsistent backgrounds."[15] The complete shift in thinking therefore required a new synthesis that would serve as a unifying basis for the special sciences. Whitehead proposed a cosmology that replaces the atomistic conception of matter with a dynamic and fluid conception of reality as processes of events, that is, energy vectors understood in terms of atomic quanta of experience.

In what follows it will be necessary to give definitions of *metaphysics* and *cosmology* for both Whitehead and Bradley. This will allow a clear understanding of their views regarding the task of the metaphysician; it will also raise important points of contrast crucial to subsequent portions of this study.

As Whitehead conceives it, *metaphysics* is "the general ideas which are indispensably relevant to the analysis of everything that happens."[16] On the other hand, he defines *cosmology* as "the effort to frame a scheme of the general character of the present stage of the universe."[17] Cosmology is distinguished by the fact that it seeks the general character of a given epoch. Its scope is limited to the type of order that dominates within that epoch. It is therefore clear that a cosmology will fall with the decline of the epoch in question. The laws of nature, for example, are not considered part of the ultimate metaphysics of the universe; they have their application only within a particular cosmic epoch dominated by particular facts. Metaphysics, however, is more fundamental than cosmology in the sense that the metaphysician seeks the general characteristics that pervade the entire universe. In such an enterprise one attempts to construct a systematic investigation into the nature of being, what Aristotle called "first philosophy" or "first principles." Whitehead viewed metaphysics as the fundamental science. In fact, for him "all difficulties as to first principles are only camouflaged metaphysical difficulties."[18] The real question is whether we pursue it in some open and systematic fashion or presuppose it in the background of our thought. Given Whitehead's own vision of the universe, metaphysics is concerned with the general features of experience, namely, his "actual occasions" which function as the ultimate constituents of a creative universe.

At times, Whitehead's use of the terms *metaphysics, speculative philosophy,* and *cosmology* seems interchangeable. Though for our present purpose it will not be necessary to distinguish between speculative philosophy and metaphysics, his cosmology is distinguished by the interpretation of actual occasions in terms of the electromagnetic characteristics of energy, and the type of order that follows—electrons, protons, atoms, molecules, cells, and so on. When we apply the generality of metaphysical notions to the present cosmic epoch we are concerned with a cosmological interpretation. However, the common denominator in all of Whitehead's later thought is the ultimate generality of process. His metaphysics provides an explanation of the rise and fall of cosmic epochs, and of various historical epochs that follow, one after another, analogous with the becoming and perishing of actual occasions.

As regards philosophic method and the evaluation of the metaphysical system, Whitehead views the ideal of speculative philosophy as a combination of both rational and empirical elements. The rational side demands that the philosophical scheme is logical and coherent with respect to the consistency and unity of ideas, while the empirical side involves the application of the scheme and its overall adequacy with respect to the interpretation of experience.

In *Religion in the Making,* Whitehead wrote that metaphysics is a description: from some special field of interest the metaphysician discerns what he suspects to be the general character of reality; he then sets up categories from this investigation and seeks to discover whether they receive confirmation by being exemplified in other fields of interest.[19] We arrive at the categories through the primary stage of assemblage. Such categories attempt to grasp the essence of the universe by the metaphysical notions of the widest extension. This provides the matrix as a body of first principles then judged as coherent and consistent depending on the manner in which each proposition requires the others in systematic interconnection. However, as a whole, the system must be confronted with the facts of experience; the final evaluation depends on its comprehensive capacity to elucidate immediate experience. In this regard, the metaphysics stands as successful given the degree to which it enlightens observations and illuminates experience in fields beyond its origin.

This method approximates the hypothetico-deductive method of scientific inquiry which Whitehead believes is shared by science and metaphysics alike. The hope of rationalism is that things lie together in a certain coherence in which no element of experience proves incapable of exhibition as an example of general theory.[20] But at the same time Whitehead is quite clear that: "Philosophers can never hope finally to formulate these metaphysical first principles. Weakness of insight and deficiencies of language stand in the way inexorably."[21] Nonetheless the scheme, as a definite statement of first principles, must be sought regardless of the emphasis placed on its hypothetical character. The metaphysician must progressively modify the working hypothesis in his approximation to the ideal scheme, for in the absence of such a well-defined scheme, Whitehead contends that "every premise in a philosophical argument is under suspicion."[22]

Whitehead says of his "categoreal scheme" that its purpose is to state the ultimate generalizations with the utmost precision and definiteness, and argue from them boldly with rigid logic. However, in Whitehead's philosophy, argument takes on more of the character of an axiomatic approach in mathematics than straightforward philosophical polemic. That is, he construes argument as a method of deriving consequences from accepted first principles or premises instead of the procedure of destroying rival schemes. This is indeed implied in his notion of metaphysics as a descriptive generalization. But this is not to say that he takes the principles asserted in his categories to be self-evident starting points from which experience is deduced. This was the mistake of Spinoza and other modern philosophers misled by the example of mathematics. Whitehead recognizes that first principles are tentative in the sense that their perfection should be the goal and not the origin of a metaphysics.

Many commentators have been critical of Whitehead's lack of philosophical argument in supporting his principles against those of rival schemes.[23] But for Whitehead the real point was to set out his system in the ideal form of an axiomatic matrix and modify it as the system evolved in various applications to special subjects.[24] Whitehead was never interested in polemic for its own sake. In fact, he thought that the persistent threat to philosophers was that polemic was becoming their chief occupation, supplanting the attempt to discover truth. The proper method of philosophy, as he saw it, is the search for the premises that extend the boundaries of previous philosophical systems and become more comprehensive with respect to the ability to describe the facts. The emphasis is placed on a "more sustained effort of constructive thought."

BRADLEY'S ABSOLUTE AND THE SKEPTICAL METHOD

Bradley was the leading Oxford philosopher of his time and the doyen among absolute idealists. Unlike Whitehead, he was originally a philosopher by training and was more straightforwardly argumentative in his approach to philosophical issues. The dominant influence on Bradley's philosophy was the neo-Hegelianism that formed in Britain against empiricism, or what Bradley mockingly referred to as "the school of Experience." T. H. Green and Edward Caird set off the movement of neo-Hegelianism, though they were eventually eclipsed by Bradley's impact on the British philosophical scene.

In spite of Bradley's protests against the spirit of "discipleship" and his dissent from membership in a Hegelian school, it is still clear that he owes much to Hegel's philosophy.[25] One of Bradley's early followers, A. E. Taylor, remarks on this point that " 'Anglo-Hegelianism' has meant in English-speaking countries, especially since the publication of *Appearance and Reality*, to all intents and purposes chiefly the views of Bradley."[26] It does, however, become clear that Bradley's work after his *Ethical Studies* moves steadily away from Hegel's influence. He himself attacks the heart of Hegelian logic, namely the dialectical process of deriving a synthesis from a contradiction.[27] Instead of viewing contradiction as a positive force in human reasoning, Bradley contends that our ability to discriminate between truth and falsehood requires that we reject self-contradiction as an accurate

characterization of Reality. What is, however, very much conso-
nant with Hegel's thinking is the notion of experience, or 'feeling,' taken from his psychology as the "vague *continuum* below
relations."[28] Bradley did see in Hegel an important basis for the
unity of the Absolute in this conception of experience.

Bradley's approach to metaphysics differs most from Whitehead in three principal ways. First, the metaphysical problem is
conceived in such a way as to expose the general principles of the
One reality, the Absolute. This is basically the monistic, as opposed to the pluralistic, approach. Second, he was not concerned
with a cosmological construction consistent with the science of
his time, nor did he attempt to integrate empirical observations in
his metaphysics. Empirical knowledge is generally assigned to the
realm of appearance; finite facts do not provide knowledge of
Reality in any ultimate sense. Bradley, in fact, would reject the
elaborate detail of Whitehead's metaphysics as excessive compared with the task of discovering a general and theoretically
tenable view of Reality. Insofar as he resists such detailed explanation of the elements of experience, he contends that his metaphysics cannot be called a system.[29] Bradley was only certain that
logic drives us to general conclusions respecting the Absolute, but
the finitude of the human condition ultimately prevents certainty
beyond a knowledge of a broad outline of Reality. Finally, from
this second point we discover a third difference from Whitehead:
It is quite clear that Bradley's general metaphysical principles are
construed as absolute foundations and not as tentative generalizations progressively modified, and judged by applications beyond metaphysics. Bradley firmly believed that metaphysics discerns absolute truth beyond all other disciplines.

As to the definition of metaphysics and its general purpose,
perhaps the most concise statement of Bradley's position occurs
on the first page of his metaphysical essay, *Appearance and
Reality*:

> We may agree, perhaps, to understand by metaphysics an attempt
> to know reality as against mere appearance, or the study of first
> principles or ultimate truths, or again the effort to comprehend
> the universe, not simply piecemeal or by fragments, but somehow
> as a whole.[30]

At first, there seems to be no disagreement between Bradley and Whitehead on these points. Both philosophers seek to know reality or ultimate truth as against mere appearance. But what exactly constitutes "mere appearance" will become an acute problem in the course of this essay. What is particularly revealing about Bradley's definition is the emphasis placed on knowing reality *as a whole*. Our being, he thinks, is a wholeness that seeks complete satisfaction. It is the metaphysician's task to consider this when constructing the main characteristics of Reality. Thus, for Bradley, we are misled when "we attempt to set up any one aspect of our nature as supreme, and to regard the other aspects merely as conducive and as subject to its rule."[31] The enthronement of one aspect of reality distorts the balance of a de facto whole, and is the very temptation of "an uncritical metaphysician." This holistic approach dominated his entire philosophical career, ethics, logic, and metaphysics inclusive.

The construction of a metaphysics involves the understanding of all that *is* in a completely self-consistent unity. This is the purely logical foundation of Bradley's metaphysics. As he put it: "Ultimate reality is such that it does not contradict itself; here is an absolute criterion."[32] With consistency as the conceptual foundation of ultimate reality, Bradley believes we arrive at truth. Imperfection and contradiction fail to be true in that they do not satisfy the demands of our whole being. Truth must be unchangeable and perfect. In *The Principles of Logic*, Bradley contends that:

> if A both were and were not, that would be because the ultimate reality had contrary qualities. The character in which it accepted A, would be opposite to the quality which excluded A from existence. Under varieties of detail we find the same basis, repulsion of discrepants.
> ... And again, if we desire to glance in passing at the metaphysical side of the matter, we may remind ourselves that the real is individual, and the individual is harmonious and self-consistent. It does not fly apart, as it would if its qualities were internally discrepant.[33]

Contradictory assertions, then, cannot be both true and representative of Reality. "The Absolute holds all possible content in an individual experience where no contradiction can remain."[34] Diversity of content is reconciled, but not contradiction.

Though Bradley attempts to steer the logical investigations of *The Principles of Logic* clear of first principles, there is the necessity of defending the axiom of contradiction as implying a certain theory of the nature of things.[35] Logic investigates the nature of inference. It is an appraisal and interpretation of what is essentially an ideal experiment on the real itself.[36] Likewise, metaphysics requires logical consistency. The assumption throughout is that Absolute Reality is without defect; this gives the metaphysician the ability to distinguish between appearance and reality by employing logic as an instrument of evaluation. With this in mind, Bradley's strategy in *Appearance and Reality* is to expose the contradictions involved in various doctrines of previous philosophical thought and show how such inconsistencies fall into varying degrees of unreality. The final result, he believes, forces us to affirm the existence of the Absolute as a perfect and individual unity.

It is often suggested that Bradley's thought is primarily negative, or based on a series of rejections and denials.[37] This is certainly a prominent feature of Bradley's method. But his thought must not be underestimated for its positive value inasmuch as his skepticism is constructive in its ultimate intent. Bradley's negative elimination by logical consistency ultimately leads to his vision of Reality as Absolute. For him there is a knowledge of what is sought with every denial. "Every negation must have a ground, and this ground is positive."[38] Philosophical skepticism, as opposed to psychological doubting, has an advantage in that it transcends itself and arrives at a more general resting place. It is distinguished by the adoption of a notion of truth and reality as the criterion of doubting. As Bradley makes the point:

> The doubt here is not smothered or expelled but itself is assimilated and used up. It becomes an element in the living process of that which is above doubt, and hence its own development is the end of itself in its original character.[39]

The "remedy against doubt" is the positive vision of Reality. It widens its area to an ultimate generality where it cannot, in theory, be transcended or refuted. Where Bradley pushes this absolutism too far, however, his arguments tend to become somewhat sophistical. His most insightful critic, William James, was indeed quick to point out how, in many cases, Bradley had produced a logic that "overintellectualized" the universe for the sake of his Absolute.[40] Bradley's dialectic, on these points, has a definite affinity to the ancients, Parmenides and Zeno. The common end sought is permanence and a vision of reality as One.

For Bradley, there is one theme that infects thought with so much contradiction that it affirms the positive character of the Absolute more than anything else. This is the central issue of relations, around which the whole of *Appearance and Reality* revolves. Bradley's critical evaluation of this topic provides a sustained attack on the basic unit of pluralism—the fact. Any relation between subjects and objects, or between terms generally, involves isolation and separation of finite facts or units of existence. But for him, this turns out to be an impossibility because it is not only impossible to discover real individuals, but even if we could tentatively identify such units, we eventually discover that their relations to one another involve us in contradictions. These arguments are so fundamental to his conclusions that he suggests, at the end of his chapter "Relation and Quality," that the convinced reader need not read the remaining chapters of Book I of *Appearance and Reality*.[41] Bradley is convinced that if one accepts the general arguments on the contradictoriness of relations, the more specific topics evaluated—the self, time, space, motion, and causation—easily fall, since they are dependent upon some type of units and relations. The point is, of course, that the problem of relations can only be resolved in a larger Whole that transmutes finite content into unity. It is here, Bradley contends, that the universe as a whole may be called intelligible.

From this it is clear how Bradley's conception of the metaphysical problem entails a specific method, and how this method attempts to reach beyond the limits of our ordinary, hypothetical and incomplete reasoning to Absolute perfection. Nothing short of the Absolute gives us the whole truth. This is the key concept in Bradley's ingenious theory of judgment where any judgment claiming to portray a genuine character of reality must fail to take account of the totality of the universe. Every finite judgment will always have a hypothetical character due to the fact that abstracted content will always fail to represent total reality. Richard Wollheim remarks on this point that for Bradley:

> Reality flows uninterruptedly, without divisions, without fissures, from one point in space to another, from one moment in time to another, and it is we thinking beings who carve it up; indeed, even the distinctions of space and time themselves are, as we shall see, importations of Thought into the realm of Reality. And in making these divisions, these breaks, we harm what is really there: our thought, which is based upon them, is therefore always a distortion of the truth.[42]

This does explain why, in Bradley's view, we can never explain the infinite detail of the Absolute or understand just how all the appearances form a systematic harmony. Where our thought formulates a judgment of the content of a given experience, it necessarily neglects the continuous mass of the Whole. This is a lesson Whitehead understood as well, but he applied it in quite a different manner in his philosophic outlook. Since, for Whitehead, the universe will always be too complex for any finite human system, the principles of a metaphysical system will only be an approximation of the general truths sought. Bradley, on the other hand, argues that logic drives us to certainty in metaphysics, provided that our principles are sufficiently general, but we will always be uncertain when it comes to various attempts to systematize finite content.

For a rough-and-ready description of their conceptions of metaphysics, I propose to view the differences between Whitehead and Bradley through a naturalized/pure distinction.[43] For this purpose, *naturalized metaphysics* means the generalizations arrived at through an assemblage of all sorts of knowledge, both empirical and conceptual. It is the traditional notion of metaphysics as the "queen of the sciences," or Aristotle's view of "first philosophy." *Pure metaphysics,* on the other hand, is a conception of a discipline, in and of itself, which, as one discipline of many and one side of our nature, contributes to our whole being. It attempts to arrive at the true nature of reality by purely *a priori* means.

According to this distinction, Bradley's conception would fall under the pure metaphysics in that he does not attempt to inte-

grate current scientific developments into his principles or anticipate the application of the principles beyond the discipline itself.
It is however clear that his intentional neglect of cosmology as
linked to the construction of metaphysical principles can be traced
to his monism and the central criticism of relations. For clearly
scientific inquiry requires an isolation of its data as well as a
strict independence of thought from the objects under investigation. Where Whitehead's pluralism provides a foundation for
scientific inquiry, articulates connections between the various disciplines, and fills the gap between natural science and value experience, Bradley argues that the respective disciplines must pursue
their own aims, each with their own methodological concerns. In
his view, any form of pluralism is an "ideal construction" for
some specific purpose at hand, and must be detached from the
metaphysician's task of knowing ultimate truth and reality. Self-
contradiction, at this level, where a discipline must isolate some
specific subject matter and investigate relations is not of genuine
interest to metaphysics. In fact, he thinks, to protest against a
particular theory of science as self-contradictory is to bring in
metaphysical criticisms at a point where they are inapplicable.[44]
This is not to say that the natural or social sciences are illegiti-
mate means of inquiry but that we must not mistake their "practical constructions" for ultimate truth. Their restriction of
attention, for a specific purpose, is necessarily limited. In his
view, the evaluation of science, and for that matter, any
hypothetico-deductive process, is always in terms of usefulness
and not of ultimate truth. As Bradley says, "The ideas, with
which it works, are not intended to set out the true character of
reality."[45] Thus, in his view, a conflict between the sciences and
metaphysics is impossible provided that we realize that they each
have their own proper sphere and function in the human intellect.

Bradley saw that science requires external relations as well as
the assumption that the inert particles of matter in time and
space are real. It was indeed obvious that the Newtonian scheme
of mechanics was useful for the practicalities of everyday life, and
in Bradley's time, there was certainly a conflict between science
and the idealist view of ultimate reality. However, at the outset of
the twentieth century, Newtonian physics lost its reign, and the
problem confronting us was the construction of a new system of

reality in which science could be understood as continuous with metaphysics.[46] A parallel controversy of the late nineteenth century that is very much characteristic of Bradley's view is the conflict between Darwinian evolution and orthodox theology. But the tenability of Bradley's view of metaphysics as separate from the scientific interests of his particular epoch is doubtful. It is hardly likely that any metaphysician can seriously claim that he was not influenced by the science of his time as well as the overall advance of knowledge and its effects on society. Surely the various disciplines have their own particular emphases and methods of achieving their aims, but the view that science is concerned only with practical constructions, as opposed to ultimate reality, cannot be taken seriously. A specific scientific discipline may be distinguished by its particular restriction of subject-matter, but this does not mean the investigation is confined to some lower level of reality.

Whitehead would agree that we must not accept as total truth any specialized system of thought limited to a restricted group of data, but he would not assign to metaphysics the sole task of uncovering the nature of reality. In this sense, Whitehead's view closely accords with the conception of a naturalized metaphysics. Metaphysics gains from the special sciences the empirical discovery of the specific features of order in the present cosmic epoch. It is therefore continuous with science via cosmology. And from the other side, science gains from metaphysics a systematic overview of fundamental concepts lying behind specialized lines of research.

Science and philosophy are merely different aspects of one human enterprise: the understanding of ourselves and the world in which we live. The real task is to find a way to think them together such that each gains insight from the other in the endless task of criticism and revision. Both begin with the same groundwork of immediate experience, and both concern themselves with the embodiment of abstract principles in concrete particular facts.

Having spelled out these differences between Whitehead and Bradley respecting their approaches to metaphysics, we shall, however, find that there are other points in common between them. Both take metaphysics as the philosophical activity that attempts to formulate the most adequate way of understanding reality in all its experienced forms. In short, they both see the theory of being (Aristotle's Being qua Being) as the fundamental problem of philosophy. Both present a comprehensive and unified worldview, and both would surely agree that the voyage of philosophy is to the higher generalities.

As to the task of the metaphysician, an insight from each will perhaps best illustrate the predicament. For Bradley, "Metaphysics is the finding of bad reasons for what we believe upon instinct, but to find these reasons is no less an instinct."[47] In Whitehead's view, the metaphysician looks for that which ordinary speech sees no point in saying, because it so pervades our experience that it is taken for granted.

CHAPTER 2

The Metaphysics of Experience

HISTORICAL PERSPECTIVE

In many respects the affinities between Bradley and Whitehead are a result of their attempts to construct a metaphysics that would overcome the problems of Cartesian dualism and its legacy in the eighteenth and nineteenth centuries. They also shared a reaction to the scientific materialism that held firm with the success of the seventeenth-century cosmology, beginning with Galileo and Descartes and culminating in Newton's grand system of physics. Bradley, in fact, identifies the dichotomy of poetry and fact, or spirit and nature, as the unnatural barrier that his metaphysics sought to break down.[1] And Whitehead's idea of process was a reconstruction of experience that would effectively eliminate the disjunction between the subjective individual experience and the objective facts of the external world, thus doing away with all of the attendant epistemological problems.[2] This was a major preoccupation of his earlier works, in which he attacked the "bifurcation of nature" by thinkers such as Descartes, Locke, and Kant. But Bradley and Whitehead were not alone in this common endeavor. Their views were formulated within a context of British and American thought that gave such problems a central place and attempted to work out solutions using a novel interpretation of experience.

Although I believe this view—which I will call the idealist doctrine of experience—was central to Anglo-American thought, at least at the outset of this century, it was in no way confined to English-speaking philosophy, for one finds aspects of it in other continental thinkers of the time. The view, however, received a rather unified and precise formulation in such philosophers as Bradley, James, Peirce, Royce, and Whitehead, particularly in opposition to the interpretation of experience common in the empiricist thought of Locke and Hume, experience primarily understood as sense experience, or the acquisition of sense data.

As opposed to this central epistemological role of experience, the idealist interpretation functioned more in the context of deciding ontological matters, especially in the attempt to overcome the problems of Descartes's two worlds of *res cogitans* and *res extensa*. Instead of postulating two radically distinct substances and then attempting to account for their interaction, these philosophers viewed the universe in terms of one ontological type, as a fusion of experience, even though they differed with respect to monist and pluralist variations. Bradley and Royce followed Hegel in their understanding of the universe as essentially One experience, the Absolute. Experience, or 'feeling', becomes the key to understanding the fusion of mind and nature; in contrast to the ordinary psychological meaning, 'feeling' becomes a metaphysical substratum where diversity is held in union. James, Peirce, and Whitehead, on the other hand, advanced pluralist versions of a universe composed of a multitude of interacting and purposive actualities forming "streams of experience." They acknowledged something more than classical empiricism's interpretation of experience as atomic sense data: Such limitations were broken down by the understanding of lived experience as phenomenologically dense. *Experience* therefore means more than "clear and distinct"; it includes the sense of valuation, beauty, aversion and attraction, and involves a crucial element of our experience of time as momentary throbs passing one to another.

In one way or another, these thinkers all showed a grasp of their own individual conscious experience, and incorporated it into a method of generalizing about the nature of reality. Experience takes on a more comprehensive role in the attempt to understand the nature and structure of the universe.

PANPSYCHISM

What pushes the idealist doctrine of experience toward panpsychism is the acceptance of the notion that all physical bodies, or their basic constituents, have a creative inner life or psychical being, regardless of our inability to discover any hint of life in what is usually classified as inanimate. It is the view that everything actual is an experience for itself. Although panpsychism does not have much of a following in current philosophical orthodoxy, the history of philosophy is indeed rich in thinkers who have adopted this view of fundamental ontology. Some of the most prominent philosophers who have held this view include Leibniz, Royce, Lotze, McDougall, Fechner, Schelling, Schopenhauer, Peirce, Schiller, Alexander, and Hartshorne. James, Bradley, and Whitehead may also be included among this group for reasons I will articulate later; albeit each of these three expressed reservations about the doctrine. Modern biologists Teilhard de Chardin, Wright, Agar, and Waddington all found the panpsychist metaphysics to be the most cogent foundation for the theory of evolution mainly because it accounts for the natural evolution of higher forms of experience out of lower and more rudimentary forms of experience.

One of the main attractions of the panpsychist theory is its ability to provide a smooth and continuous interpretation of the world in terms of the same ontological type. In this regard, Leibniz is the paradigm case of panpsychism in modern philosophy. He was one of the first philosophers to have seen the defects in the Cartesian system, and proposed a way to overcome the difficulties of both dualism and materialism in his *Monadology*. Having looked within his own mind to discover the monad, Leibniz found a continuous process of activity that he termed "perception." As he says: "The passing condition, which involves and represents a multiplicity in the unit or in the simple substance, is nothing but what is called Perception".[3] From this point, Leibniz generalizes that every real being is essentially active, and whatever does not act does not exist. Hence the simple substances, the monads, are the ultimate units of force in the universe; they act according to their own internal nature, and physical bodies must be understood as aggregates or compounds of these psychical unities.

Leibniz obviously refused to admit any such distinctions as living versus nonliving, or man versus animals, as ultimate. The broad jumps between the various forms of existence disappear as the world of nature stretches along a continuum from the lowest to the highest forms of life—mineral, vegetable, and animal—with imperceptible shadings from one form to its neighboring form. What appears to be inert and lifeless to us is simply the limiting case at the lower end of the continuum. These are the simple, unconscious monads. But as we move up the continuum to more complex forms of life, we find more sophisticated monads that involve various degrees of feeling and consciousness until we arrive at human consciousness, and ultimately, God.

Royce has continued this argument with a most challenging contribution that slightly modifies Leibniz's doctrine. For Royce, it is not the case that the apparently inanimate or inorganic is unconscious. It is rather a consciousness utterly unintelligible to human perceivers. In this view, the whole of nature is the expression of meaning and conscious fulfillment of significance in life. In his major work, *The World and the Individual*, he writes:

> Where we see inorganic Nature seemingly dead, there is, in fact, conscious life, just as surely as there is any Being present in Nature at all. And I insist, meanwhile, that no empirical warrant can be found for affirming the existence of dead material substance anywhere. What we find, in inorganic Nature, are processes whose time-rate is slower or faster than those which our consciousness is adapted to read or to appreciate.[4]

What is actually different among the various manifestations of finite individuality is the apperceptive timespans experienced. Our anthropocentric tendencies force us to conclude that our apperceptive span is the only possible one. But Royce argues that there is an infinity of experiences other than ours that are characterized by special apperceptive spans.[5] It may be that, for a consciousness having the same content as ours but which has a different apperceptive span, what seems to us to last a second is stretched out into a series lasting an entire era.

Although the experience of different durations of time among different manifestations of Being remains fundamental in Royce's system, we should not conclude that communication is only possible among those that share the same apperceptive spans. This would indeed be contrary to the most positive principles of Royce's ontology, where intercommunication and cooperation among finite individuals form larger wholes. For Royce, *communication* simply means the interdependence of life in the arteries of Being.

When James considered panpsychism in his *Principles of Psychology*, his attention was drawn to the position by the way it accounts for continuity in the theory of evolution. He writes:

> We ought ... ourselves sincerely to try every possible mode of conceiving the dawn of consciousness so that it may *not* appear equivalent to the irruption into the universe of a new nature, non-existent until then.
>
> ... Consciousness, however little, is an illegitimate birth in any philosophy that starts without it, and yet professes to explain all facts by continuous evolution.
>
> *If evolution is to work smoothly, consciousness in some shape must have been present at the very origin of things.* Accordingly we find that the more clear-sighted evolutionary philosophers are beginning to posit it there.[6]

But having articulated the position with such eloquence, James himself was not completely committed to it in the *Principles* or in his later work. In fact, he seems to oscillate between panpsychism and phenomenalism in his philosophy of radical empiricism where he held the view that reality is comprised of events that are intrinsically neither psychical nor physical but potentially either or both. Yet it is difficult to regard his concept of 'pure experience' as anything other than the *"consciousness in some shape,"* or at least experience of the same *kind* to which all realities whatsoever must belong. At times he reads as if he is committed to the position; at other times he seems more skeptical. The same can be said of Whitehead. But in many respects, the commitment to panpsychism seems to be more of a verbal dispute than anything else. Whitehead, for example, unlike Royce, thought that consciousness was not fundamental but rather arose from a more rudimentary basis of experiencing actualities. If he wavered on the question of panpsychism, it seemed to be really just a matter of clarifying whether the doctrine committed him to the view that consciousness is fundamental. If so, then he was not a panpsychist; otherwise it appears there is good reason to view him as such.

In the past, the most serious objection to panpsychism has been an alleged inability to do justice to the hard facts of physical science. The idea that an electron behaves as it does as a result of various interactions of sentience inherent in the sub-subatomic particles has, for obvious reasons, been unenlightening to the physicist whose task involves objective measurements and predictions. Few will doubt the legitimacy of this objection provided that the scope of the physicist's investigations are defined in terms of describing and measuring physical phenomena. However, given that one is seeking answers to the question of the fundamental ontology of the world, the panpsychist view has definite advantages over a purely materialist ontology. One advantage, as James clearly found, is that it does not slip in some entirely new nature that was not already there from the beginning. And indeed, it is rather difficult to understand how "the lights go on" at some stage of evolution when consciousness is thought of as an emergent property of certain purely physical systems. In this regard, it is more plausible to think of consciousness as emergent from a basis that shares some of the same properties rather than none at all. Secondly, as opposed to the Newtonian and thermodynamic paradigms that describe the universe as either a sterile machine or in a state of generation and decay, the panpsychist view provides a more intelligible basis for the notion of a creative universe that emphasizes the progressive, organizational aspects of nature.

When Leibniz recognized the difficulty of making use of such metaphysical principles in science (i.e., that the real explanations are psychical), he insisted on a thoroughgoing mechanism in physics and physiology, even though the only real forces are appetitions, desires, emotions, or purposes. Science, he thought, must approach the world in terms of apparent rather than real forces and describe and explain phenomena rather than the inner life of monads. This view also continues in Bradley's thought when he argues that science deals with abstractions or appearances rather than with Reality. The situation today, however, has changed somewhat since quantum mechanics and the theory of evolution are hardly mechanical in the sense that Newton, Leibniz, or Bradley understood physical science. But this does not mean that science now studies the ultimate units of experience, whatever they may be: monads, finite centers of experience, or actual occasions. Depending on the particular scientific specialization, what is studied is the behavior of the aggregates formed by such units. For example, physicists will be interested in the subatomic realm of electrons, protons, and the various effects of fission, fusion, etc. Chemists will see molecules as their basic units where chemical behavior depends essentially on the arrangements of the smaller units, namely, atoms and electrons. And biologists will investigate the behavior of cells and genetic inheritance in living organisms.

From here the continuum enlarges as the subject matter of science expands—plants, animals, man, societies, planets and galaxy clusters. But at the most fundamental level, metaphysical or ontological investigations attempt to articulate the basic units of reality that enable a coherent and comprehensive view of interconnections.

In our own time, the paradigm for science has been the electromagnetic features of energy, and with this, Whitehead clearly saw that the time was ripe for a reconciliation between science and a metaphysics of experience. In this respect, his cosmological construction attempts to explain extension and temporal succession as derivative from the momentary character of actual occasions. Once mass as a quantity of matter was displaced by mass as a quantity of energy, events and happenings became fundamental, and simple location in time and space was replaced by vectors and electromagnetic fields.[7] Of course this observation in itself does not show that panpsychism is somehow vindicated by modern science. But for Whitehead it seemed that the science of his time was moving away from a purely materialist ontology and that an ontology of events, to which science seemed to be pointing, was more compatible with panpsychism.

Aside from Whitehead and the attempts of various biologists, most thinkers that have proposed a panpsychist metaphysics have not been attracted to the notion for its scientific merits.[8] It is also quite clear that, from the point of view of common sense, panpsychism seems contrary to our basic beliefs about much of the extended world. But what common sense assumes is that the failure of our perceptions to discover sentience, individuality, or activity in the inanimate implies their absence from these parts of nature. Indeed, subatomic physics now describes a world in which the inanimate is full of energetic vibrations and complex individuation. But the actual discovery that the whole of nature is fundamentally sentient will forever elude the grasp of scientific knowledge and common sense.

It seems fairly clear that we can imagine some sort of rudimentary experience that goes on in the most simple creatures. As Timothy Sprigge has recently put this point, this is to understand "things in themselves" or the noumenal nature of physical reality as opposed to an abstract conception of the structure of physical things or a phenomenal description.[9] But the lower we descend on the continuum of nature, the less likely we are to imagine the kind of concreteness such organisms experience. Though where we make the exact cut is rather arbitrary, once we go below the animal kingdom to organisms that do not seem to have a dominant centre of experience, our capacity for empathy fades. That is, having human experience as our only possible standard, our capacity to understand in detail the type of experience that goes on in lower organisms fades from realization.

BRADLEY'S FINITE CENTRES OF EXPERIENCE

The central role of the concept of 'feeling' in Bradley's metaphysics is characteristic of idealist reactions to scientific materialism. For Bradley the abstract entities described by physical science could never be substituted for our full concrete experience of reality as one continuous whole. It is only when we pass away from this primitive harmonious unity to a knowledge of related things, of thought, analysis, and judgment, that we pass from what might be called a state of preconceptual innocence to the flawed world of contradiction. Such a departure from immediacy, from the infrarelational level of experience to the relational level of thought, is certainly a necessary aspect of human life. However, Bradley insists that we must realize how this process will always involve a distortion of reality.

Bradley's thought, on many points, has a clear affinity to Wordsworth's poetic expression of the revolt against scientific materialism. Wordsworth's dictum "we murder to dissect" is reiterated by Bradley's "analysis is the death of feeling"; for analysis will always involve an abstraction from the continuous mass of felt experience. In an early formulation of this concept, Bradley writes:

> It is a very common and most ruinous superstition to suppose that analysis is no alteration, and that, whenever we distinguish, we have at once to do with divisible existence. It is an immense assumption to conclude, when a fact comes to us as a whole, that some parts of it may exist without any sort of regard for the rest.[10]

At the moment analysis takes place, we have taken one step back from what is actually present in immediate feeling as the intellect discerns objects and qualities. The whole background from which abstraction is accomplished is neglected as the preconceptual union of feeling gives way to analysis and an endless web of relations. Reality thus fractures into parts and pieces. The problem, however, is putting it back together in such a way as to insure that nothing has been altered. But Bradley clearly recognizes the impossibility of this task. We are no longer referring to concrete reality, but rather to isolated aspects cut from its harmonious texture. In fact, at this point, we are working within the realm of appearance, and the manipulations of abstracted content fall into various degrees of truth and reality.

Bradley's doctrine of degrees of truth and reality involves the notion of a continuum stretching from the fully concrete Reality, the Absolute, whose contents are nothing but sentient experience, to abstract entities, such as those postulated by scientific materialism. At one end of the spectrum, we approach the Absolute through the unity of feeling where no contradiction remains. But the more we depart from feeling and affirm the independence of finite entities, the more we approach the relative unreality of a lifeless and abstract matter. Though Bradley does not undertake an exact system, showing how the various aspects of appearance fall into their proper places on the continuum, he does provide this general formula:

> You may measure the reality of anything by the relative amount of transformation, which would follow if its defects were made good. The more an appearance, in being corrected, is transmuted and destroyed, the less reality can such an appearance contain; or, to put it otherwise, the less genuinely does it represent the Real.[11]

Hence, the more an appearance tends toward internal unification and feeling, and the less it is transformed when corrected, the more reality it contains. But let us now consider, in some detail, what 'feeling' means in Bradley's metaphysics.

Thus far we have considered 'feeling' as a unifying principle where we directly encounter Reality. We have seen that it must be (i) preconceptual (i.e., before immediate experience has been analyzed into objects and qualities), (ii) nonrelational, and (iii) devoid of contradiction. But what exactly is this primitive activity at the base of all experience?

We should first discard any association with mere sensation, in other words with the feelings of pain, pleasure, grief, or affection. Bradley clearly says that "Feeling here naturally does not mean mere pleasure and pain; and indeed the idea that these aspects are our fundamental substance has never seemed, to me at least, worth discussing."[12] 'Feeling' must therefore be more fundamental and pure; yet it must not "be taken as simply one with any 'subliminal' world or any universe of the Unconscious."[13] Nor should we identify 'feeling' with consciousness. Clearly 'feeling' is wider in the sense that there are many influences, of which we are not conscious, that melt imperceptibly into our totality of experience. For the most part Bradley uses *feeling* and *immediate experience* interchangeably, as when he writes: "I use, in brief, immediate experience to stand for that which is comprised wholly within a single state of undivided awareness of feeling."[14] Or again: "Feeling is immediate experience without distinction or relation in itself."[15] Yet it is not synonymous with experience in the general sense, for relational experience comprises a great many degrees of appearance resulting from the very departure from immediacy. And neither is 'feeling' to be equated simply with the Absolute experience. 'Feeling' points the way to Reality, but Reality itself is not 'feeling'.

Bradley's clearest conception of 'feeling' is put forth in his essay "On Our Knowledge of Immediate Experience." It is here that the notion of a diversity of content felt as a unity, the many-into-one concept, appears as fundamental to his metaphysics.

According to Bradley then, feeling is a unity, yet it remains complex in its internal diversity of content. It is "an awareness which, though non-relational, may comprise simply in itself an indefinite amount of difference."[16] In 'feeling' there are no relations or terms present as the whole of experience comes as the immediate unity of the psychical centre. Knowing and being become one in 'feeling'. There is no distinction between the subject of experience (that which feels) and the objects of experience (that which is felt), as such divisions clearly involve the *relation* of knower to known. As we have seen above, such distinctions are abstractions or ideal constructions cut out of the harmonious texture of immediate feeling. Bradley makes this point in *Appearance and Reality* when he writes: "Experience in its early form, as a centre of immediate feeling, is not yet either self or not-self. It qualifies the Reality, which of course is present within it; and its own finite content indissolubly connects it with the total universe."[17] From this perspective, the self, subject, or the I of the experiencing relation has not yet emerged as a distinctive entity. It is simply fused with the diversity of content in one mass of felt continuity. Equally, on the other side of the relation, the not-self, or objects of experience, are in a nebulous and undistinguished state as not yet consciously focused to attention. The many are felt as one; there is only pure being in an undisturbed and undivided unity.

Though it is somewhat difficult to disabuse ourselves of the prejudice that feeling is something subjective and private, and thus only affects the subject, and not what is properly felt, we find that this dualism dissolves when, following Bradley, we understand 'feeling' to be the very basis of experience that sustains the subject-object, self–not-self relation. As Bradley writes: "Feeling is the beginning, and it is the source of all material, and it forms the enfolding element and abiding ground of our world."[18] It fills the divided chasm left blank by Descartes's dualism.

Clearly the self is not the basic experiencing unit, but it should be obvious that the many-into-one function occurs within some type of entity. Bradley calls the basic units in which 'feeling' occurs "finite centres of experience," and conceives of them as the constituents of the Absolute. Initially it seems that the admission of finite centres to his metaphysical outlook conflicts with his radical monism. This, however, only applies to the notion of a plurality of *independent* entities which Bradley never claims for his finite centres. We must keep in mind that the Absolute does have focal points through which Reality shines in all its rich and varied manifestations. But for Bradley the finite centres are neither completely independent nor are they considered truly real, for ultimately they are conceived as special appearances of the Absolute. How, exactly, this is accomplished is beyond finite understanding. Nonetheless Bradley contends that they are necessary conceptions "without which we could not express ourselves, and through which alone we can formulate that higher truth which at once contains and transcends them."[19]

A clear grasp of Bradley's use of the concept of finite centres is crucial in order to understand how the many-into-one theme functions at several levels in his philosophy. But, unfortunately, Bradley himself is rather obscure in his use of the term. It may therefore help to distinguish between an 'enduring' and a 'momentary' sense of the finite centres of experience.[20] Although Bradley does not actually use these terms, his discussion in various places implies that what we call the 'momentary centre' may be understood as an aspect of the 'enduring centre'. In a reply to a criticism by James Ward, for example, he says that there is "a serious difference between finite centres on the one hand and mere aspects of one centre on the other hand."[21] Also, Bradley sometimes uses the term "prolonged finite centre" which approximates what we shall here call the 'enduring centre'.[22]

Enduring centres of experience are the focal points of the Absolute. One particular centre may be said to be enduring in the sense that it is the character that is always felt to be the same as it becomes unified with some particular content (e.g., the unchanging character of a centre throughout the various stages of a person's life).[23] On this point, T. S. Eliot describes Bradley's finite centres as especially close to Leibniz's monads. He writes: "I suggest that from the 'pluralism' of Leibniz there is only a step to the 'absolute zero' of Bradley and that Bradley's Absolute dissolves at a touch into its constituents."[24] Indeed we need only refer back to Leibniz's view of monads as indestructible psychical unities and his theory of perception as "multiplicity in the unit" to see the similarity. Just as Bradley's finite centres have momentary appearances, Leibniz's unchanging monads have modifications that appear in temporal succession. From this point of view, Bradley's finite centres are very close to souls. But in a later essay entitled "What is the Real Julius Caesar?" he makes certain qualifications:

> A soul is a finite centre viewed as an object existing in time with a before and after of itself. And further the soul is a thing distinct from the experiences which it has, which experiences we take not as itself but as its states.[25]

Here we find Bradley making the same sort of distinction that he made between the self and finite centres. The soul must be an entity distinct from the experiences it has. On the other hand, the finite centre of experience cannot be distinguished from its experiences. It is its experiences and nothing else. And, as Bradley says, it cannot be understood as existing in time. "It is temporal in the sense of being itself the positive and concrete negation of time."[26] The enduring centres fill that portion of the Universe in a timeless eternity. This gives him the notion that the finite centres of all persons—past, present, and future—contribute the richness of diversity to the Absolute, even though the portions that they fill may not overlap or coincide in a temporal sense.[27]

Aside from the enduring character of finite centres, Bradley also thinks that their momentary aspects (i.e., their appearances in time) are how we come to know something of their enduring character. What we perceive as process in time is the perpetual shifting of content from existence, and, at any one moment, the finite content becomes an immediate unity with existence. In the essay on "Immediate Experience," we find Bradley's vivid characterization of our psychical life as momentary pulses. For example, he writes:

> In any emotion one part of that emotion consists already of objects, of perceptions and ideas before my mind. And the whole emotion being one, the special group of feeling is united with those objects before my mind, united with them integrally and directly though not objectively.[28]

The finite centre, in this sense, unifies the diversity of content—of objects, perceptions, and ideas—as one emotion in a certain temporal quantum. But the momentary centres must be understood as aspects of the enduring centre, as notes are to a melody. Bradley, on this point, says that the enduring centre "can contain a lapse and a before and after, but these are subordinate."[29] It is only by a breach of the eternal presence of the enduring centre that we are able to understand how the emotion of any one moment contributes to the life of the centre. And the sense of time and continuance gained from meditating on this momentary character remains essentially ideal.

It is rather perplexing that Bradley calls his basic units of experience "finite," if ultimately he conceives of them as the eternal, or timeless, qualifications of the Absolute. We must, however, understand 'finite' to mean finite content taken into the wholeness of experience. In *Appearance and Reality*, Bradley focuses attention on the distinction between the 'this' and the 'what' of experience. For example, he explains: "Reality is being in which there is no division of content from existence, no loosening of 'what' from 'that.' "[30] Variety of content and the momentary character of 'thatness' are the finite aspects that qualify the whole feeling.

Perhaps this will help us to understand a further point of some difficulty. Though nothing, in the end, is real but what is felt in the immediate unity of the finite centre, we must not therefore understand any of this to be equated with Reality. This would be a fundamental error in interpreting Bradley. In fact, at several places, he stresses the self-transcendent character of feeling that may be said to result from the internal collision of the 'what' with its 'that'. The finite form of 'thisness' and its specious unity are always short-lived and must pass beyond into something higher and more comprehensive. As he puts the point:

> For the finite content is necessarily determined from the outside; its external relations . . . penetrate its essence, and so carry that beyond its own being. And hence, since the 'what' of all feeling is discordant with its 'that', it is appearance, and, as such, it cannot be real. This fleeting and untrue character is perpetually forced on our notice by the hard fact of change. And, both from within and from without, feeling is compelled to pass off into the relational consciousness. It is the ground and foundation of further developments, but it is a foundation that bears them only by a ceaseless lapse from itself.[31]

It is this very fleeting and ceaseless lapse of momentary feeling that Bradley thinks cannot, in the end, be taken as truly real. In spite of the apparent self-completeness, the "this," the very throb of existence, is always a member of a wider whole. The immediate feeling is always a more remote fringe of experience that is at once "the assertion and negation of *my* 'this'."[32]

Bradley's view of the self-transcendence of 'feeling' has not only been the central focus of disagreement with James, it has also been, in large measure, an issue of much misunderstanding with critics of his philosophy.[33] But the importance of 'feeling', for Bradley, is that it is the ground and starting point for metaphysical inquiry, though it is not to be taken as the end, or thought of as identical with Reality. The nonrelational many-into-one unity of 'feeling' is our low and imperfect example of what must be the case at the level of the Absolute.[34] In short, the immediate unity of the finite centre supplies us with the basic principle which, if developed to a final self-completion, will provide the general character of the suprarelational experience.[35] At most, our own example must be taken as analogical with the activity of the Absolute where all experience is harmonized into one final moment of eternity.

Within this basic context of 'feeling' and finite centres, panpsychism seems to fall easily into place. However, Bradley stops short of committing himself to the doctrine. It is a possible option for his metaphysics but is considered unnecessary to complete his general conception of the Universe.

Given Bradley's view that Reality is nothing else but sentient experience, one could easily take him to be advancing a doctrine of panpsychism similar to that of Leibniz or Royce. "There is," he declares, "no being or fact outside of that which is commonly called psychical existence. Feeling, thought, and volition . . . are all the material of existence, and there is no other material, actual or even possible."[36] But just exactly what this comes to requires closer examination.

In the chapter entitled "Nature" in *Appearance and Reality*, Bradley says: "Abstract from everything psychical, and then the remainder of existence will be Nature."[37] It does, however, soon become clear that there is no such remainder. He quickly dismisses the possibility of an inorganic Nature on the grounds that there could not exist an arrangement that somehow escapes or lies outside of the experience of the Absolute.[38] But the crucial issue is whether the things of nature are all psychical in character, and whether the whole of nature is arranged by the volition of finite centres of experience. Since this is a genuine possibility for Nature, Bradley remains open. However he does think that it is beyond our capabilities to discover whether this is in fact the case. He says that our failure "to discover these symptoms is no sufficient warrant for positive denial," and footnotes the panpsychist, Fechner, in this connection.[39] Indeed, Bradley here realizes that arrangements of "personal unities" could very well be organized within the Absolute and be "directly connected with finite centres of feeling." And granted this, what is perceived as the common world with a certain uniformity of nature is a result of the will of the Whole.[40]

On the other hand, Bradley's argument against panpsychism comes at several points where he entertains the question: "Is there any Nature not experienced by a finite subject?"[41] Or again: "Is there . . . in the universe any sort of matter not contained in finite centres of experience?"[42] If it is possible that there are various aspects of the universe that are not reflected through finite centres, then panpsychism is unnecessary. This would not make those aspects unattached, just unmediated or unfiltered. Such aspects would still consist of experience, ultimately absorbed into the Absolute, but they would not be matter perceived by us as nature. The fact that they are not filtered through finite centres makes them possible only for the Absolute where they are experienced directly.

Bradley takes this question seriously because of his conviction that the details of Absolute life completely escape the capabilities of finite intelligence. As he says:

> We do not know why or how the Absolute divides itself into centres, or the way in which, so divided, it still remains one. The relation of the many experiences to the single experience, and so to one another, is, in the end, beyond us. And, if so, why should there not be elements experienced in the total, and yet not experienced within any subordinate focus?[43]

An affirmative response to the question of panpsychism, then, would seem to involve an understanding of details in the Absolute that would exceed his central task of discovering the main features or general principles of the Universe.

Though Bradley avoids dogmatism by giving equal weight to both sides of the argument, I suspect that he recognizes that a commitment to panpsychism would push him far too close to a pluralistic metaphysics. Presumably he is rejecting an interpretation of the world in terms of very low levels of sentience that would place too much emphasis on the momentary centres. But if we take him as denying the possibility of panpsychism, it is not at all clear just why finite centres should be confined to human beings. Certainly the difficulty here is just where to make the exact cut in nature between what does and what does not have a centre. But in the end, it seems that an affirmative response to panpsychism is wanting despite his claim that our "miserably incomplete" knowledge of Absolute life makes this impossible to determine.

WHITEHEAD'S ACTUAL OCCASIONS

Although Whitehead's doctrine of experience has many different sources synthesized into his novel formulation, we shall only be concerned here with his affinity to Bradley.[44] At later points, however, it will be necessary to consider other influences in order to determine exactly where Whitehead's view diverges from Bradley's.

The explicit statement of his conformity to the idealist doctrine of experience comes as a major principle in the categoreal scheme of *Process and Reality*, the "ontological principle," which states that, outside of the experience of actual occasions, there is absolutely nothing. Whitehead summarizes by saying, "no actual entity, then no reason."[45] Actual entities or actual occasions are the final real things in the universe; there is no going behind them to discover anything more real. They are the most concrete units of reality from which all other types of entity are derived by abstraction. Whitehead, like Bradley, therefore insists on a return to the concrete, and has attempted to build a philosophic system based on that which is immediately present in experience. His well-known "fallacy of misplaced concreteness" is, in fact, a protest against philosophic or scientific schemes that attempt to build systems based on the more abstract things and then arrive at the more concrete things. In this regard, mechanistic materialism is Whitehead's prime example of a theory that mistakes the abstract for the concrete because it represents the world in terms of instantaneous configurations of matter. But the trouble is that there is no such *experience* of the world in this manner, thus the whole conception is a high abstraction.

For Whitehead, the clearest instance of an actual occasion is to be found in a moment of one's own consciousness. In fact, the actual occasion is best conceived as a metaphysical generalization of an initially psychological concept.[46] Introspection reveals the concrete drop of experience; this then becomes a method for generalizing about the rest of the universe. As he describes his "working hypothesis" of *Process and Reality*, he writes:

> if we hold . . . that all final individual actualities have the metaphysical character of occasions of experience, then on that hypothesis the direct evidence as to the connectedness of one's own immediate present occasion of experience with one's immediate past occasions, can be validly used to suggest categories applying to the connectedness of all occasions in nature.[47]

Given this procedure, Whitehead believes that the puzzle as to the connectedness of nature is solved by appealing to the texture of life that is always right before us. The final actualities are all alike; they are all natural units of process, of becoming and perishing. But compared to the infinite multitude of actualities that constitute nature, the actual occasions that make up human consciousness are highly specialized instances. Such occasions are the "crown of experience" and are best understood as derivative from a more rudimentary and fundamental level of process.[48] This is where Whitehead and Bradley connect.

Whitehead contends that the very base of experience is a continuous flow that is essentially primitive and unconscious. It is simply a momentary throb of 'feeling' where objects and subjects, qualities and relations, remain undistinguished. Bradley understood this to be the preconceptual unity of 'feeling' where experience is essentially undivided and nonrelational. In Whitehead we find an analogous doctrine with his notion of "perception in the mode of causal efficacy" where 'feelings' are "vague but insistent." What we perceive in this type of experience is a very dim sense of the compulsion of the immediate past forcing itself into the present and continuing into that novel moment. Causal efficacy is the sense of the presence of the past that is localized yet evades local definition.

The continuity of experience is the key notion here. As opposed to the very clear and distinct perceptions of the world that Whitehead calls "perception in the mode of presentational immediacy," causal efficacy conveys the most basic fact of existence, namely, passage. Where presentational immediacy supplies the details of sensa, such as our keen visual perceptions, causal efficacy supplies the continuity of experience, and it so pervades our experience that we hardly take notice of it. It is therefore understood as the persistent inheritance of brute givenness, of the massive presence of the past in the process of merging into the present. The 'feelings' it transmits are vague, inarticulate, and simply felt as the efficaciousness of the past. Whitehead, on this point, writes:

> Such feelings, divorced from immediate sensa, are pleasant or unpleasant, according to mood; but they are always vague as to spatial and temporal definition, though their explicit dominance in experience may be heightened in the absence of sensa.[49]

Of course where evolution has given us acute receptors, such as our highly developed sense organs, we naturally focus attention on the clear and distinct sensa of presentational immediacy. But, as Whitehead suggests, in the absence of such sensa, we encounter reality at a level that remains at bottom and fundamental. Our dim consciousness of half-sleep, the thumping of our heartbeat, and the visceral feelings of well-being all suggest continuous becoming in the mode of causal efficacy.

Such crude perceptions must be as close as we can come to understanding what the rest of reality is like. What we experience when we meditate on this process of becoming is analogous to the experience of lower forms of life that do not possess such refined organs of sense. Whitehead thus argues that the variety of organisms that exhibit modes of behavior directed toward self-preservation suffice as evidence of feeling and causal awareness with the external world. He writes:

> A jellyfish advances and withdraws, and in so doing exhibits some perception of causal relationship with the world beyond itself; a plant grows downwards to the damp earth, and upward towards the light. There is thus some direct reason for attributing

dim, slow feelings of causal nexus, although we have no reason
for any ascription of the definite percepts in the mode of
presentational immediacy.[50]

The point, of course, is that the whole of existence must have a
very primitive awareness of causal efficacy that lies at the base of
reality.

Whitehead effectively argues that most modern philosophers,
in their analyses of perception, have ignored perception in the
mode of causal efficacy by concentrating on those distinct impressions mainly revealed through visual perception. The obvious
result is that they have attempted to analyze perception solely in
terms of presentational immediacy, and have had continuous problems with regard to the continuity of experience. Hume's view of
impressions, for example, takes the data of presentational immediacy as primary, but then finds that such data do not disclose
any causal influence. The conclusion of an analysis in the mode
of presentational immediacy is that events in the contemporary
world are causally independent of one another. It unveils the
world at an instant, and, if taken in itself, will not reveal any
intrinsic connection with the past or future.

The fundamental contrast between causal efficacy and presentational immediacy was captured succinctly in Russell's recollection of an argument with Whitehead. Speaking of his own philosophy, he writes:

> It was Whitehead who was the serpent in this paradise of
> Mediterranean clarity. He said to me once: "You think the
> world is what it looks like in fine weather at noon day; I think
> it is what it looks like in the early morning when one first
> wakes from a deep sleep." I thought this remark horrid, but
> could not see how to prove that my basis was any better than
> his.[51]

Russell, like Hume, held a doctrine of external relations where
independent objects and isolated qualities were fundamental to
his logical atomism. But what he perceived in Whitehead's view
that caused some difficulty for his own was the essentially dumb
force of causal efficacy. In waking from a deep sleep, for example, one experiences consciousness coming more clearly into

focus and the data of presentational immediacy becoming more acute. But in the first few moments, one has a sense of reality in its most basic form.

The real deception of Russell's logical atomism is that our language, with its distinct words for separate objects and qualities, provides an adequate grasp of the basis of reality.[52] Language, of course, naturally attunes itself to presentational immediacy. But the subject-predicate structure of language has a peculiar difficulty when it comes to expressing the 'feelings' of causal efficacy. It can only grasp a particular distinctness that lingers after the fact.

Whitehead was quite insistent on the inadequacy of the subject-predicate structure of language throughout his philosophical career. His main criticism of modern philosophy is the recurring problem of taking the subject-predicate form of statement as conveying a truth that is metaphysically ultimate.[53] It has a sound pragmatic defense, but in metaphysics the concept is sheer error. In Whitehead's view, language was designed for the marketplace; it has pragmatic justification in that it serves our immediate purposes, but it does not capture the essence of reality. This was the very reason why Whitehead found it necessary to invent terms such as *actual occasion, concrescence,* and *prehension* to express the fluid-like character of process. But one of the results of his use of these neologisms is that his thought has been regarded as highly obscure by the more orthodox schools of twentieth century philosophy.

Whitehead's view of reality puts him at one with Bradley in at least three important senses: (i) the rejection of the "vacuous actuality" as an instance of reality devoid of experience, (ii) the rough correspondence between his view of perception in the modes of causal efficacy and presentational immediacy with Bradley's view of 'feeling' in terms of existence and content, and (iii) the attack on abstraction as an accurate portrayal of reality.

First, both Whitehead and Bradley clearly accept the general notion that there cannot be any part of reality that is not made up of experience. Both would therefore embrace the maxim "to be is to experience." For Bradley, Reality finds expression through finite centres of experience, that is, Reality is the synthesis of experience. And as we have seen with Whitehead, the actual occasion is the most concrete unit of experience and the fundamental building block of the universe.

Second, the basic parallel with Bradley's "that" and "what" of experience is obvious. Momentary centres, like actual occasions, are made up of both existence and content. On the one hand, we have the sense of thatness of experience, namely, our intuitive grasp of the continuity of experience. And on the other hand, we have the specific content, the data of sense, which are contained in the facts of passage. Neither can be truly separated from the other, but in conscious analysis it is possible to make such distinctions. For both Whitehead and Bradley, as long as we dwell in the realm of clear and distinct qualities and spatial relations, (i.e., within presentational immediacy alone), we will remain on a fairly abstract level of thought that deals with isolated objects in purely external relations. It is this, Bradley says, that loosens the "what" from the "that" and removes us from the preconceptual immediacy of 'feeling'. Similarly, for Whitehead, such a one-sided analysis of experience will never supply any information as to our primary perception of the connectedness of experience.

This brings us directly into our third point of contact. With 'feeling' as the basis of reality, we must not be deceived by the apparent completeness of any statement that abstracts from the totality given in any one experience. Though Whitehead does not have an explicit doctrine of degrees of truth and reality, he does suggest something very close to this when he discusses "half-truths," and the notion that our finite judgments make the total truth quite inaccessible.[54] That is, the truth *sub specie aeternitatis* is quite impossible for the human beings. Conscious discrimination and analysis zeros in on those clear and distinct details given in any one totality. But such a process and the resulting judgment about those facts must be regarded as highly abstract. We can never do justice to the harmonious unity that is there in 'feeling'. As Whitehead says in his very late work, *Modes of Thought*: "These relations, thus abstracted require for their full understanding the infinitude from which we abstract. We experience more than we can analyze. For we experience the universe, and we analyze in our consciousness a minute selection of its details."[55]

Though it would be misleading to suggest that, at this level, the parallels between Whitehead and Bradley are complete, we do have a point of contact for the interpretation of 'feeling' in their respective philosophies. Whereas the discrepancies will be dealt with in the following chapters, at present, we focus on broad similarities in their metaphysical views. There is, however, one crucial difference that must be brought to surface before proceeding to consider the essential characteristics of the actual occasions and to compare them with Bradley's finite centres of experience.

Whitehead says that his philosophy of organism is an inversion of Bradley's doctrine of actuality. Instead of regarding the actual occasion as a mode of a more genuine Individual, the Absolute, the occasion is the final reality. Whitehead's finite units of fact are the genuine individuals of the creative process, whereas for Bradley, the finite facts are indeed present in process, but they are taken as imperfect modes of one perfect and all-embracing Absolute. Whitehead writes: "The final actuality is the particular process with its particular attainment of satisfaction. The actuality of the universe is merely derivative from its solidarity in each actual entity."[56] Whitehead thus clearly rejects Bradley's claim that the individual moment of experience is inconsistent if taken as fully real. This rejection also explains why Whitehead considers 'feeling' to have a particular emotional tone depending on the character of each actual occasion.

As a consequence of this fundamental contrast, Whitehead's view of Bradley has focused solely on the momentary centre of experience. Much of this comes clearly to surface when he quotes directly from Bradley's essay on "Immediate Experience."[57] This means that Whitehead has purposely neglected some of Bradley's most important points regarding the self-transcendence of 'feeling' and the relative unreality of the fleeting moment. Furthermore, there is nothing in Whitehead's metaphysics that corresponds to the enduring centre of experience. In other words, there is no eternal and timeless centre like the Leibnizian monad. The actual occasion is a quantum of sheer becoming, and thus

Bradley's understanding of 'feeling' as a metaphysical substratum is rejected. The whole subject-object relation in Whitehead's view becomes a temporal concept, namely, the relation of present to the past, and 'feeling' is reinterpreted as a process of objectification.

What Whitehead does find in Bradley's theory that accords so well with his own reflection is the notion that, at the base of experience, this continuous process of the many becoming one is achieved by 'feeling'. If we keep in mind Bradley's essential point regarding the diversity of content felt as a unity at the level of the momentary finite centre, we shall find much agreement in both thinkers. Compare, for example, the following passage from Whitehead, which takes on a distinctive Bradleian tone:

> Each monadic creature is a mode of the process of 'feeling' the world, of housing the world in one unit of complex feeling in every way determinate. Such a unit is an 'actual occasion'; it is the ultimate creature derivative from the creative process.[58]

Although Bradley does not describe his finite centres as creative in any sense, the basic point is clear. Each actual occasion becomes a complex unity by feeling the world and by including the diversity of content within itself. Whitehead calls this function of the universe "creative" because it involves an activity of synthesis. This is the most general and comprehensive principle of Whitehead's metaphysics, the "Category of the Ultimate," which states that at each successive moment, "the many, which are the universe disjunctively, become the one actual occasion, which is the universe conjunctively."[59] Each actual occasion becomes a novel synthesis by 'feeling' the disjunctive diversity of its immediate past. Life is thus born anew with each conjunctive unity. The present occasion transforms what is settled in the antecedent universe as it actively selects from the multitude of data.[60] It creates with what is given, namely, the objects of the immediate past, to produce in its subjective immediacy a new entity that will become an object for the future.

At some points, Whitehead uses *feeling* in a very general sense, giving the suggestion of life operating in every single actuality throughout the universe. It is here that Whitehead adopts Bradley's term with approval and says that "this whole metaphysical position is an implicit repudiation of the doctrine of 'vacuous actuality'."[61] Without a doubt, Whitehead accepts Bradley's claim that 'feeling' is the beginning and the source of all material forming the enfolding element and abiding ground of our world. It is the essential defining characteristic of each and every actuality whereby the many become one. But at other times, Whitehead's use of *feeling* takes on a much more specific and technical meaning than we find in Bradley's metaphysics. This is not to say that it is inconsistent with Bradley's meaning, but that it is much too detailed for the general scheme put forth by Bradley. In this sense of the word, Whitehead defines a 'feeling' as a "positive prehension," which means an uncognitive apprehension of the data of the past. It is consistent with Bradley in the sense that it literally means to grasp onto the data of the world, and to include those characteristics within its present unification. Such data become internally related in the present experience. But it is certainly a modification of Bradley's doctrine in that Whitehead has described prehension as the most concrete mode of relatedness forming the component elements of actual occasions. He therefore insists, contrary to Bradley, that relations are present below the level of consciousness and make up the very fabric of 'feeling'. On this point, Whitehead also distinguishes a negative prehension which finds no parallel in Bradley. This is the activity of eliminating characteristics or data that are incompatible with the aim of the present occasion. The data are considered but not included in the particular determination of the occasion in question.

Throughout this chapter we have seen how both Bradley and Whitehead reject the materialistic and dualistic approach to metaphysics in favor of a comprehensive ontology of experience. Here the affinities have been very general. But in our examination of these affinities, we have also discovered certain qualifications of Bradley's doctrine in that Whitehead has placed greater emphasis on the novelty of creative choice and the reality of the temporal process. Such considerations mark a fundamental contrast and will occupy much of our attention in the following chapters.

CHAPTER 3

The Analysis of Experience

INTRODUCTION

In the first two chapters, we brought to the surface the basic context of metaphysical principles common to Whitehead and Bradley. In this chapter we shall analyze the contents of immediate experience in a more or less psychological framework. This analysis will draw out some of the basic contrasts between the two thinkers and then function as a basis to explore Whitehead's interpretation of Bradley.

The very fact that we attempt a detailed analysis of experience does become rather problematic for our comparative study, for clearly there is nothing in Bradley's philosophy that corresponds to the exhaustive analysis of 'feeling' central to Part III of Whitehead's *Process and Reality*. In explicit contrast to Bradley, Whitehead says: "The elucidation of immediate experience is the sole justification for any thought; and the starting-point for thought is the analytic observation of components of this experience."[1]

As discussed above, the intricate detail of Whitehead's system far exceeds any such discussion in Bradley's metaphysics. As Bradley makes it clear, his aim in metaphysics is a general and theoretically tenable view of reality that does not require a detailed explanation of all aspects of the Universe. Such a scheme, he thinks, is quite impossible for finite beings. Furthermore, we must keep in mind that, for Bradley, any analysis of 'feeling' results in its destruction. He explicitly says that 'feeling' "does not offer itself as intelligible."[2] What is left, once analysis has cut into its harmonious unity, is not Reality but abstractions and contradiction.

With respect to Bradley's first point, it is clear that, for him, philosophy itself is a finite and imperfect attempt to describe the infinite perfection of the Absolute. But if we simply substitute *universe* for *Absolute*, we find that Whitehead was no less humble. In fact, Whitehead repeatedly criticized the attempt to encapsulate the universe in any one system. "Philosophy," he says, "is the attempt to express the infinity of the universe in terms of the limitations of language."[3] This was the very reason why he conceived the proper method in metaphysics to be hypothetico-deductive. Still, Whitehead's recognition of the limitations of finite systems did not constrain his own attempt to provide a detailed metaphysics of experience. For Whitehead the point is to be as systematic and precise as possible in attempting to grasp the complexity of the universe but, at the same time, never imagine that the system has any kind of finality.

As to the second point regarding the problem of analysis, we seem to be faced with a more serious objection. If 'feeling' in the more general sense refuses to satisfy the demands of intelligence, Whitehead's project appears to be extremely problematic. But this is precisely the point where Whitehead and Bradley depart. Whitehead argues that causal efficacy, i.e., the rudimentary and vague sense of becoming, is not open to the type of clear and precise analysis in the mode of presentational immediacy. But it is nonetheless analyzable since consciousness does discern individual units of becoming, and at this level of abstraction, the occasions are genetically analyzable into phases of the concrescence and into individual prehensions which are themselves analyzable.[4] At this level Whitehead holds that more specific metaphysical principles can be formulated, and that these must apply to all occasions in nature.[5] That is, since our experience derives from a natural world of throbbing actualities, what is discerned at the level of consciousness must be seen as a highly illuminated version of the basic stuff of becoming, even though "consciousness only dimly illuminates the prehensions in the mode of causal efficacy."[6]

But the real problem confronting us now is the problem of how the continuous tissue of experience can be made up of a sequence of discrete quanta of experience. We have seen that, for Bradley, this is not Reality but an ideal construction. For him, a process of individuals is a departure from the sense of feeling as a continuous undivided harmony. This problem brings us right to the concept of the "specious present"—an old controversy between Bradley and James.

THE SPECIOUS PRESENT

In his pioneering work, *Principles of Psychology*, James revolutionized our understanding of experience by concentrating on our perception of time. At the outset of the chapter entitled "The Perception of Time," he addressed the question "What is the *original* of our experience of pastness, from whence we get the meaning of the term?"[7] We commonly divide the course of time into past, present and future, but the *"prototype of all conceived times is the specious present, the short duration of which we are immediately and incessantly sensible."*[8] James, following E. R. Clay, attacked the idea that the present can be an instantaneous flash between the immediate past and future. "Let any one try, I will not say to arrest, but to notice or attend to, the *present* moment of time."[9] Indeed it is only as an "ideal abstraction" that such a notion is possible. What is experienced, however, is a short duration in which some elements are experienced as past, some as present, and some as about to occur in an ongoing flow of experience. With characteristic clarity, James writes:

> the practically cognized present is no knife-edge, but a saddle-back, with a certain breadth of its own on which we sit perched, and from which we look in two directions into time. The unit of composition of our perception of time is a *duration*, with a bow and a stern, as it were—a rearward—and a forward-looking end. It is only as parts of this *duration-block* that the relation of *succession* of one end to the other is perceived. We do not first feel one end and then feel the other after it, and from the perception of the succession infer an interval of time between, but we seem to feel the interval of time as a whole, with its two ends embedded in it.[10]

According to James, then, the specious present is a duration-block or an observed unity that realizes itself as the totality of its temporal parts. The present is "specious" in the sense that it is never just here-now. It is, rather, a temporal stretch that overlaps and includes bits of the past as well as anticipations of the future. But the important point to keep in mind is that there are definite quanta discerned by consciousness and felt as whole moments. This is the essential psychological basis for James's later metaphysical theory, his radical empiricism, in which the "drops of experience" become the basic units in a pluralistic universe. All forms of existence must be understood as either extracts cut out from these pulses or wholes composed of a number of them woven together by their felt transmission.

Though James recognized such definite units of experience, he placed equal emphasis on the continuity between them. Each pulse is an experience for itself, but also feels its continuity in a "stream of experience." The divisions between the moments of consciousness are not sharply separated from one another but rather flow together with such ease that we hardly notice a difference.[11] But surely, when we reflect on the specious present of any one moment, it is not the same one of the moment past. Each drop has its own character and duration, and each fades as a novel drop continues where it left off.

Bergson too must be mentioned in this connection since he held a view remarkably close to that of James when he advocated the use of intuition, as opposed to intellectual analysis, as the only means of unveiling the flowing stream of reality. Intellectual analysis, he thought, would give, at best, a science that portrayed reality as instantaneous, deterministic cross sections. But the concept of a homogeneous time series is a pure abstraction, only useful for scientific investigations where it becomes an independent variable. Bergson, like James, held that reality has no such measurably neat divisions. But Bergson emphasized the flow of reality to a greater degree than any type of connectedness of units.

The metaphors of "running water," "drops," and "streams" to depict reality were natural associations for these philosophies of process, and perhaps these images best capture the event character of experience. Just as the multitude of drops melt together to form a flowing stream, innumerable throbs of emotion melt together to form the natural rhythms of our experience. The feeling is not one of a solid substance, but rather a very fluid and rushing stream.

Bradley had advanced a criticism of the instantaneous and homogeneous concept of time well before both James and Bergson in *The Principles of Logic.* He is, however, quite opposed to any attempt to break up our psychical life into any type of individuation, and is therefore unwilling to settle for anything less than a continuous whole. Bradley insists that there is only the unity of 'feeling', not 'feelings'.[12] And here we must keep in mind that his own finite centres, so far as they exist as objects and endure in time, are made and subsist only by ideal construction.[13]

For Bradley, our tendency to set up the momentary appearance as atomic and individual is pragmatically necessary but mistaken insofar as we take such constructions to be fully real. Any attempt along this line will lead us right into the endless web of terms and relations. Though we must refrain from plunging straight into these arguments here, his analysis of the problems surrounding the specious present does demand our immediate attention.

In *The Principles of Logic*, Bradley takes up the problem of discerning the individual moment of time in order to locate the subject of an analytic judgment, that is, a judgment in which the idea refers to what is given in immediate perception. But when we attempt to isolate *the present*, we are unable to discern the subject due to our inability to grasp any unit of experience clearly identified as *the present*. As a temporal phenomenon, the present either has no duration and time at all, or we discover that the duration itself has a temporal diversity that would result in an infinite regress of nows. Bradley argues:

> For no part of space or time is a final element. We find that every here is made up of heres, and every now is resolvable into nows. And thus the appearance of an atomic now could not show itself as any one part of time. But, if so, it could never show itself at all. Or, on the other hand, if we say the appearance has duration, then, like all real time, it has succession in itself, and it would not be the appearance of our single now.[14]

Like James, Bradley agrees that the concept of an instantaneous present is a pure abstraction. Atomic instants do not occur in immediate experience. But as we can clearly see from this passage, Bradley rejects the duration as an atomic individual as well. Any attempt to locate an individual, other than the one universal Individual, is an abstraction from that continuous whole present in 'feeling'. To make this point more clearly, Bradley entertains the stream metaphor in an attempt to show the inadequacy of the concept of the specious present. Even though this was eight years before the publication of James's *Principles of Psychology*, and the term *specious present* is not explicitly mentioned as the target of his attack, it does become quite clear that he is rejecting any picture of the given as an event with fixed boundaries marked by similar events on either side. As Bradley begins this thought experiment, he writes:

> Let us fancy ourselves in total darkness hung over a stream and looking down on it. The stream has no banks, and its current is covered and filled continuously with floating things. Right under our faces is a bright illuminated spot on the water, which ceaselessly widens and narrows its area, and shows us what passes away on the current. And this spot that is light is our now, our present.
>
> We may go still further and anticipate a little. We have not only an illuminated place, and the rest of the stream in total darkness. There is a paler light which, both up and down stream, is shed on what comes before and after our now. And this paler light is the offspring of the present.
>
> . . . The result, which at present we have wished to make clear, is that the now and here, in which the real appears, are not confined within simply discrete and resting moments. They are any portion of that continuous content with which we come into direct relation. Examination shows that not only at their edges they dissolve themselves over into there and then, but that, even within their limits as first given, they know no repose.[15]

So for Bradley, the illuminated spot on the stream is simply an image meant to show our inability to extend the reality that lies on either side of it. It is our limited scope through which we view the Real, but must not itself be taken as real.

What is rather odd about his interpretation of this thought experiment is the fact that he does not see the subject in question as immersed in the rushing flow of the stream, but merely observing what is passing on it. This contrasts with James's "stream of experience" in the sense that Bradley's observer and the stream are not identical. But still this does not affect his main point that we must not take what is present in the momentary appearance as the sole reality. Reality continues far beyond what we experience in any one moment.

At times, Bradley makes observations that seem to accord with the concept of the specious present. For example, in the same passage just quoted, he says: "The appearance is always a process of disappearing, and the duration of the process which we call our present has no fixed length."[16] This suggests agreement with James regarding the heterogeneous character of the drops of experience. But special care must be taken on this point. Where James understands the duration as an experienced unity of temporal parts, Bradley argues it is an infinite regress of nows. The present, for him, is the filling of that duration in which Reality appears and can therefore only be regarded as the negation of time. That is to say, Reality does not exist in time; it only appears there and creates the fiction of an atomic now.[17]

Having seen how James and Bradley approach the problem of the specious present, we now turn to Whitehead, who, in my view, provided the most convincing solution in his theory of "epochal becoming." But before we examine Whitehead's solution to this problem in his later metaphysical works, we require some preliminary background from his earlier investigations in the philosophy of natural science.

In *The Principles of Natural Knowledge*, and in the less technical exposition of these views presented in *The Concept of Nature*, Whitehead devoted much of his attention to the problems of our perception of temporal passage and spatial relatedness in order to discern the ultimate data for natural science. Much of his critical analysis focused on the concept of an instantaneous and homogeneous time, the traditional Newtonian view of time as flowing equally in measurable lapses. This is the source of all our difficulties of physical explanation; for if such a concept of instantaneous nature is accepted, our science must 'abandon all claim to be founded upon observation.'[19] Nature at an instant does not exist for sense-awareness; it is simply a pure abstraction useful in physics where we are permitted to speak of the universe at times t_1, t_2, t_3, and so on.

In his philosophy of natural science, Whitehead proposed that the ultimate units that characterize the creative advance of nature should be events. This, he held, was the only way out of the confusion; for our perception of time is as a duration, and within this duration we can always discriminate constituent events. Our recognition of events, and the objects situated in these events, occurs within the ultimate datum for sense-perception, the spe-

cious present.[20] Here Whitehead, like James and Bergson, appeals
to what he calls "instinctive," or "naive" experience, as opposed
to the intellectual theory of time as a moving knife-edge. The
apprehended event must be the content of a specious present of
some observer. This is obviously the only way in which events
and their objects could be known; for within the duration, the
passage of nature is retained.

By choosing events as the ultimate constituents, Whitehead
wished to demonstrate the very rich and diverse aspects of nature. Nature does not happen as clock time, but rather as experienced time, and this comes in duration-blocks or stretches of
varying lengths. The event, he says, is "the most concrete fact
capable of separate discrimination."[21] It is never merely in time,
but always constitutes a four-dimensional continuum of space-
time, and is therefore never limited to the instantaneous
present. The point-instants that are crucial to physical explanations are understood only as ideal and are arrived at by
Whitehead's novel "method of extensive abstraction"—a progressive narrowing of perceptible durations whereby the logical limit
is reached.[22]

At various points in The Concept of Nature, Whitehead's
discussion of our perception of time cannot fail to remind us of
James.[23] Also he says: "We may speculate . . . that this alliance of
the passage of mind with the passage of nature arises from their
both sharing in some ultimate character of passage which dominates all being."[24] This is, however, a speculation Whitehead had
not worked out in his philosophy of natural science. In fact, he
explicitly says that this is the very distinction that separates natural philosophy from metaphysics.[25] What we must keep in mind
is that his earlier investigations are concerned only with the object side of the knowing relation, even though some psychological
speculation was necessary in order to explain his theory of events
and the concept of cogredience. But at the outset of The Concept
of Nature, Whitehead anticipated much of his later thought when
he said that "the values of nature are perhaps the key to the
metaphysical synthesis of existence."[26] And indeed the concept of
the actual occasion was exactly what was required in order that
the events of nature, the physical world, take on the same charac-

teristics as the specious present of the observer apprehending those events.

In Note II (written in 1924) to the second edition of *The Principles of Natural Knowledge*, Whitehead said of the first edition (1919) that "the true doctrine that 'process' is the fundamental idea, was not in my mind with sufficient emphasis."[27] In this book there is little indication as to how events become and pass away. We know that they overlap by whole-part relations and connect together by temporal ordering, but the manner in which they penetrate and carry their objects is not fully developed. These are considerations that are beyond the scope of the early works; but much of the detail does become clear by the time Whitehead advanced the idea of the actual occasion and the relation of prehension, both of which appeared to develop out of the theory of epochal becoming.[28] Once events are given an atomic structure, the extensive structures of the world are seen to grow out of the manner in which individual occasions achieve a real togetherness in nature. A pluralistic temporal atomism thus replaces the earlier system of whole-part layering of events.

In *Process and Reality*, the "actual occasions" are closely related to the earlier "events," and "eternal objects" to the earlier "objects." The exact relationship between these two pairs of entities is a difficult problem. But aside from the addition of the subjective nature of actual occasions, the important point to bear in mind is that an event becomes a nexus of actual occasions in the metaphysical works. The nexus is a succession of actual occasions forming our experience of continuity and change. What we perceive as change is the differences between the individual characters of the occasions forming such an event.

Whitehead agrees with James in his analysis of continuity by adopting the idea that the individual units of experience must come in "whole moments" or "epochs."[29] Each occasion of experience becomes a whole, not in pieces that complete a whole. On this issue, Whitehead takes Bradley's infinite regress argument to be a serious threat to becoming and to the whole notion of temporal atomicity. Although he mistakenly refers to Zeno's arrow paradox on this matter, it is quite clear that he intends to refer to the argument of the dichotomy, which produces the same conclusion as Bradley.[30] Whitehead explains his own version of the argument as follows:

> Consider, for example, an act of becoming during one second. The act is divisible into two acts, one during the earlier half of the second, the other during the later half of the second. Thus that which becomes during the whole second presupposes that which becomes during the first half-second. Analogously, that which becomes during the first half-second presupposes that which becomes during the first quarter-second, and so on indefinitely.[31]

So, if the present moment that we call "now" is divisible into an indefinite number of "nows," then the paradox of becoming is a vicious infinite regress which proves that nothing can become. However, if the occasion of experience, as a perceptible amount of change, comes all at once, then there is no longer any mystery about becoming. For Whitehead, temporalization is the realization of a complete organism, the realization of some definite spatio-temporal quantum.

What has been established by Bradley and Zeno is that there cannot be a continuity of becoming.[32] Time cannot be a continuous unfolding of portions or acts of becoming mainly because any particular portion or act can be divided further. As Whitehead makes it clear in another essay, the paradox arises as a result of combining two incompatible notions—supersession and continuity.[33] Continuity is therefore rejected as a metaphysical feature of the occasions of experience. They come all at once or not at all. This is the basis for atomism in Whitehead's theory. In the succession of the unit becomings or epochal wholes, what becomes is continuity. Thus Whitehead writes:

> The conclusion is that in every act of becoming there is the becoming of something with temporal extension; but that the act itself is not extensive, in the sense that it is divisible into earlier and later acts of becoming which correspond to the extensive divisibility of what has become.[34]

Though the act of becoming is not continuous, extensive, or in physical time, it delivers a definite temporal quantum to the world. The act must therefore happen in a quasi-temporal realm Whitehead calls the "genetic process." He emphasizes that "the genetic process is not the temporal succession: such a view is exactly what is denied by the epochal theory of time."[35]

To illustrate Whitehead's point, let us consider a diagram of moments composing an event (see figure 1). In the succession of occasions, *A, B, C,* and *D,* each occasion becomes an epochal whole and forms the continuity of time.

Figure 1

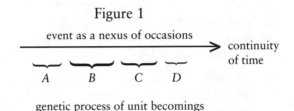

In this diagram, *A, B, C* and *D,* taken together, form an event of perceptible change in the world. The uneven lengths in the continuity represent the heterogeneous character of the occasions. But the continuity of time presupposes the genetic process that underlies our perceptual experience of events. Our experience of time as a continuous whole is therefore constituted by the discontinuous succession of atomic, epochal becomings.

Bradley, as we have said before, approximates such explanations of the unity of feeling as whole epochs of becoming. In his *Essays on Truth and Reality,* for example, he defines immediate experience as "that which is comprised wholly within a single state of undivided awareness or feeling."[36] And again in *The Principles of Logic,* he writes: "If we are content to take the facts as they come to us, if we will only leave them just as we feel them, they never disappoint us."[37] Indeed "just as we feel them," they are undivided unities becoming and passing away from the present into the past. But it is clear that, for Bradley, there is no becoming and perishing. What he means is that the universe happens as one epochal Whole, and in 'feeling' we have some grasp of how this unity is accomplished. In his view, he therefore denies that 'feeling' can be a genuine plurality. This is where the real difference occurs between Whitehead and Bradley. The crucial point concerns how the whole units of 'feeling' are linked together to form our continuous experience. Bradley continues:

> They neither hang by these airy threads from the past, nor
> perish internally in a vanishing network of never-ending relations
> between illusory units. The real, as it comes to us in sense, has
> nothing of all this.[38]

And in an explanatory note on temporal and spatial appearance
Bradley wrote in the second edition of *Appearance and Reality*:

> all this birth and death, arising and perishing of individuals, is
> it ultimately true and real or is it not? For myself, I reply that it
> is not so. I reply that these successive individuals are an
> appearance, necessary to the Absolute, but still an appearance.[39]

But in Whitehead's view the intuitive feeling of transition is none
other than an awareness of our experience of the immediate past
as having perished yet still remaining as part of the present. Here
some type of relatedness between the moments must be admitted
if we hold that the facts that compose our experience are whole
units that become and pass away. Although I shall touch on this
below, detailed examination of the arguments must be reserved
for the following chapter. For the present let us return to the
analysis within any one moment of experience, that is, given that
some sort of pluralism is tentatively admitted.

GENETIC ANALYSIS AND THE
COMPONENT ELEMENTS

Now that we have seen how genuine individuals are possible for
Whitehead, we investigate the component elements of his actual
occasions. As I mentioned at the outset of this chapter, the analysis of the activity within one occasion of experience is a highly
abstract procedure in Whitehead's metaphysics. But for him, such
an analysis is essential to give a detailed explanation of the fluency
of the actual world.

Once again we are concerned with the activity whereby the
many become one. This is the problem, Whitehead says, that the
concrescence solves.[40] "The analysis discloses operations trans-
forming entities which are individually alien into a complex which
is concretely one."[41] Analysis discovers that the occasion is *many*
things by virtue of the complexity of feelings or prehensions constituting its existence. In this respect, the occasion is divisible into

component parts. But if something is divisible, it does not necessarily follow that it is divided. As an epochal whole, the occasion is *one* thing, synthesizing the many elements into an undivided unity by its subjective aim, the final cause of the process of growth. Indeed it is in virtue of this subjective aim that the occasion produces one entity.

So we have the notion that the actual occasion is a cell by virtue of the vast complexity of prehensions, but at the same time, an undivided atomic unity by virtue of its subjective aim. Though the feelings may be many, there is only one concrete unit of experience.

In the attempt to explain the process of concrescence and the manner in which an occasion acquires its data, we should keep in mind Whitehead's fundamental distinction between two ways of considering the actual occasion: the "genetic" and the "morphological" analyses. Above we have seen a trace of this distinction when we touched on the genetic process that underlies our perceptual experience of continuity. Genetically, we are concerned with the various elements of the universe from which the occasion arises. These are: (i) the actual occasions felt, (ii) the eternal objects felt, (iii) the 'feelings' felt, and (iv) the subjective forms of intensity. In addition, these elements involve the various phases of selection and elimination of such data. Morphologically, we are concerned with the completed actual occasion, spatialized and functioning as an object for subsequent prehensions. In this respect it is said to be the terminal unity of the concrescent process because it has perished. This is what Whitehead calls "satisfaction."

Perhaps another way of explaining the difference between genetic and morphological analyses is to say that the former is microscopic while the latter is macroscopic. One is concerned with the formal constitution of the actual occasion while the other is concerned with the givenness of the actual world considered as "stubborn fact." In this section, I will be attempting to clarify Whitehead's analysis of the genetic process, and though, largely expository, this section will be an important point of reference for subsequent chapters of this comparative essay.

The concrescence of an actual occasion is the process of growing together with the other occasions that have already achieved satisfaction in the temporal process. A completed concrescence is an occasion that has become concrete in physical time. Within this concrescence, there is a process of moving from the spark of subjective immediacy, where the antecedent universe is synthesized into a novel arrangement, to the satisfaction and the completed object. But at this point it must be made clear that Whitehead's use of the term *object* does not mean an enduring substance. When an occasion functions as an object in the process, it is a possible choice for the subjective immediacy of subsequent occasions. Accordingly, Whitehead uses the neologism *subject-superject* in an attempt to avoid confusing his doctrine with the traditional conception of subject and object. He says:

> An actual entity is at once the subject experiencing and the superject of its experiences. It is a subject-superject, and neither half of this description can for a moment be lost sight of. The term 'subject' will be mostly employed when the actual entity is considered in respect to its own real internal constitution. But 'subject' is always to be construed as an abbreviation of 'subject-superject.'[42]

So the subject is the occasion's private experience while the object, or superject is to be understood as the public outcome or completion of the concrescence. Whitehead thus construes the subject-object relation not as static and confined to the present but as a temporal relationship that emphasizes the activity of becoming and perishing. The subject experiences the objects of the immediate past to form its own synthesis, a superject, itself to become an object for future occasions.

For the sake of clear exposition, I shall first discuss the concrescence as two phases: the initial phase and the supplemental phase. Then I shall break down the supplemental into three stages of activity, namely, conceptual 'feelings', simple comparative 'feelings' and complex comparative 'feelings'.[43]

Generally, as the concrescence moves to its satisfaction, there is a passage characterized by a passive reception of the antecedent universe to an active selection of the data from which it forms the novel individual. The origin of the concrescent process is the multiplicity of data that enters into the present actuality and becomes elements of its own internal constitution. The initial phase is said to be "passive" or "conformal' in order to express the way in which the multitude of data enter into the subjective immediacy of the occasion without any selection that affects the final outcome. This phase is merely receptive as the past merges into the present. At this point, the initial prehensions are purely physical prehensions; they are simple physical or causal 'feelings' that merely conform to what is settled in the past. The following supplemental phase, on the other hand, is an active process of self-creation. From the multitude of data felt in the conformal phase, the occasion now molds itself by selection and elimination. The data that are "positively prehended" are taken into the constitution of the present actuality as compatible with its subjective aim. Such elements have value for the occasion and become its essential ingredients. Those elements that are not part of this selection are called "negative prehensions." They are eliminated from this particular determination even though they may be positively prehended by other contemporaries. The main point for any one occasion, however, is that the achievement of its aim will always involve elimination. This gives the occasion its particular character and makes possible a novel individual in the universe.

In Whitehead's view, the data that are positively prehended by an actual occasion obtain "objectification" in that occasion. The individual facts absorbed into the internal constitution of the subject achieve an "objective immortality" beyond their perishing in the immediate past. They are, so to speak, reenacted in the life of the present moment. This is essentially what Whitehead means when he says, "The philosophy of organism is mainly devoted to the task of making clear the notion of 'being present in another entity.' "[44] The present must include the past with some degree of definiteness. This distinguishes his view from a mere representative theory of perception, and constitutes a major divergence from modern philosophers such as Descartes and Locke. But it should be clear that no actual occasion survives as a whole beyond its present immediacy; only its individual prehensions become objectified as each successive moment of the universe moves from disjunction to conjunction.

In certain respects, this principle of selection and elimination is very close to Leibniz's notion that each monad mirrors the entire universe by the combination of its clear and confused perceptions of all the other monads. Leibniz was also concerned with a principle in which certain properties define an individual. But, unlike Leibniz's monads, Whitehead's actual occasions have a momentary existence, and the defining characteristics of such occasions are elements of past occasions. Since Leibniz's monads are modeled on the subject-predicate form of proposition, the logical argument that the predicate is contained in the subject led Leibniz to deny the interaction between substances. But as we saw in chapter 2, the subject-predicate form of proposition was explicitly rejected by Whitehead as a foundation for metaphysics. With this in mind we might also add that Whitehead was very much thinking of process in terms of the theory of evolution. In fact, his concepts of prehension and objectification can be regarded as generalizations of genetic inheritance in biology. Where, in the metaphysical doctrine, the emphasis is placed on the elements compatible with the subjective aim of the occasion, the upshot in biology is the adaption of an organism by natural selection.

Finally, to complete our discussion on these general factors of the concrescence, we must consider the "subjective form," which is *how* the occasion 'feels' its data. This involves the inheritance of a certain emotional tone from the immediate past. It is *how* the character of the prehending subject conforms to the character of the 'feeling' of the datum. Subjective form supplies an essential aspect of continuity to experience, and manifests itself in the concrescent process in various species such as emotions, valuations, purposes, adversions, and aversions.

Whitehead distinguishes between different types of entity that constitute the data of the antecedent universe. Thus far the term *data* has been employed in the loose and somewhat vague sense of "everything that is available for prehension." But Whitehead is quite clear about the various types of entities, and the manner in which they become incorporated into the present. This involves the supplemental phase of the concrescence.

In the supplemental phase, Whitehead distinguishes two stages: one of "conceptual feelings" and another of "comparative feelings." The latter may be divided further into "simple" and "complex" comparative feelings thereby giving us three final stages.[45]

Whitehead also says that there is a twofold aspect of the creative urge operating within the phases of the concrescence. The actual occasion has two poles, the mental and the physical. But despite this unfortunate choice of terms, we must not take this dipolarity to mean anything like a mind-body division within each occasion. Whitehead himself later regretted that he had chosen these terms.[46] Also we must be quite clear not to confuse the mental pole with consciousness. It involves valuation but not consciousness.

Where, in the phases of the concrescence, Whitehead is thinking of linear or horizontal phases, he now adds a vertical dimension of poles that prehend the data.[47] In our discussion thus far we have considered the physical pole of the occasion where throbs of emotional energy are transferred from one moment to the next. In the conformal phase, what is purely physical inheritance of this emotional energy is, in the supplemental phase, essentially accompanied by creative or aesthetic synthesis. This is the activity of the conceptual 'feelings' via the mental pole of the actual occasion. These 'feelings' have eternal objects as their data and, unlike the physical 'feelings' that must conform to the immediate past, they can simply dismiss the eternal objects as unnecessary for the final satisfaction.[48] Again, in the conformal phase, the physical pole has absorbed the nexus of actual occasions clothed in the specific forms of definiteness, the eternal objects. Whitehead says that the mental pole starts with the conceptual registration of the physical pole, and then reacts to what has entered into its subjective immediacy. This is where conceptual choice takes place, and the eternal objects of the past are now molded to fit the ideal of the occasion's subjective aim. But what is particularly unique about the mental pole is its ability to entertain alternative possibilities in abstraction from their particular mode of realization. It has the ability to introduce something new from the welter of atemporal potentials, that is, some form of definiteness not yet realized in the temporal process. As Whitehead puts it:

> The mental pole introduces the subject as a determinant of its own concrescence. The mental pole is the subject determining its own ideal of itself by reference to eternal principles of valuation autonomously modified in their application to its own

physical objective datum. Every actual entity is 'in time' so far as its physical pole is concerned, and is 'out of time' so far as its mental pole is concerned. It is the union of two worlds, namely, the temporal world, and the world of autonomous valuation.[49]

An actual occasion reproduces the ingredient eternal objects in the physical prehensions, but it can also introduce novelty for future prehensions via the activity of the mental pole. Hence we find that this stage of the concrescence is indispensable to the activity of self-creation. Otherwise there would be nothing new.

Another qualification must be added. Whitehead has also found it necessary to introduce a principle of dominance to the poles so that actual occasions can differ in terms of the relative importance of the mental pole. This means that there is an intensity of valuation where there is a dominance in the mental pole, and a lack of such activity in occasions that have a dominance in the physical pole. The multitude of actual occasions that make up a stone, for example, have a dominance in their physical poles, and a negligible amount of activity in the mental poles. With little change from day to day, year to year, there is simply an inheritance of the eternal objects present in the physical prehensions, and little expectation of a novel addition to this inheritance.

Although we have omitted from our discussion some of the essential theological considerations involved in the conceptual 'feelings,' we should mention here Whitehead's view that the subjective aim is supplied by God's ideal of what is possible in the occasion's immediate situation. He provides the lure for the best outcome, although, in the end, there is an autonomous decision by the mental pole as to how far it will be realized.

We now move on to the next two stages of the concrescence, which apply to actual occasions with a dominance of the mental pole. In *Process and Reality*, these stages come under the chapters entitled "Propositions and Feelings" and "The Higher Phases of Experience," and in certain instances, they involve the more special occasions of human consciousness specifically in the last stage of intellectual 'feelings'.

At the end of the stage involving conceptual 'feelings,' if a new eternal object has been introduced in the concrescence, it must, in some way, be integrated with the inherited physical 'feelings.' This is accomplished by what Whitehead calls "comparative feelings," of which there are two general types. These are distinguished as stages of "simple" and "complex" comparisons, or comparisons and comparisons of comparisons. Here the prehensions are "impure" or "hybrid" because they are prehensions of pure prehensions, both conceptual and physical. These last two stages move the concrescence toward further unification since the comparison of the mental and physical poles produces an integration of their data into the novel one.

A simple comparative 'feeling' holds in the unity of a contrast a simple physical 'feeling' from the conformal phase and a conceptual 'feeling' from the supplemental phase. The conceptual 'feeling' here is normally the counterpart of the physical 'feeling' derived from it by conceptual valuation. This means that there is a comparison of what was physically felt with what was conceptually felt in terms of an "integrated datum" or "generic contrast" in the concrescing subject of this stage. There are two types of simple comparative 'feelings', namely, "physical purposes" and "propositional feelings." The physical purposes terminate at this stage since they occur in the more primitive actual occasions that inhibit further integrations. The propositional 'feelings' are considered an evolutionary development out of physical purposes and provide a lure for further integration.

With physical purposes, what is felt is a contrast between the fact of the physical 'feeling' and the valuation of a transcendent eternal object embodied in the conceptual 'feeling'. The eternal object was originally taken from an earlier stage of the concrescence. But at the present stage, the eternal object that is considered merely sinks back into immanence in the physical 'feeling'. The result is that the datum ceases to be a lure for 'feeling' for the present occasion, and the concrescence of the subject terminates because the initial physical 'feeling' of the subject is simply reiterated. Generally, this stage of physical purposes is the stage in which the transmission of 'feeling' from one occasion to the next gains a stability that makes "enduring objects" possible; it is the stage where there is an "association of endurance with rhythm and physical vibration."[50] The propositions, on the other hand, are the "lures for feeling, and give to feelings a definiteness of enjoyment and purpose which is absent in the blank evaluation of physical feeling into physical purpose."[51] They mark a stage of

existence between the physical purposes and the conscious purposes of intellectual 'feelings'. The contrast involved here is between the nexus of actual occasions, termed the "logical subject,"
and the complex eternal object forming a "predicate." But the
eternal object is a pure abstract possibility, and thus remains
transcendent and indeterminate even though it has its character enhanced. In the proposition, it is always a "sheer fact as a
possibility."[52]

If a proposition has been felt in the stage of simple comparative 'feeling', an intellectual 'feeling' may arise in the final stage
of the concrescence. As Whitehead says: "In an intellectual feeling the datum is the generic contrast between a nexus of actual
entities and a proposition with its logical subjects members of the
nexus."[53] This he calls the "affirmation-negation contrast"—a
contrast between what is in the actual world and what is sheer
possibility, transcendent and indeterminate. On the one hand,
there is the nexus of actual occasions as objectified in the physical
'feeling', and on the other hand, there are the possibilities, what
might be, namely, the lure of the proposition. This is "the contrast between 'in fact' and 'might be,' in respect to particular instances in this actual world."[54] As we have seen, the proposition
itself is already a comparative 'feeling'. So now we have a comparison of that comparison, and this is the intellectual 'feeling'.

Though we shall not require a detailed examination of
Whitehead's theory of judgment connected with the intellectual
'feelings', we should take notice of the importance of the subjective form that occurs as a result of this final contrast. This is, in
fact, the stage where consciousness arises. Whitehead says:

> The subjective form of the feeling of this contrast is con-
> sciousness. Thus in experience, consciousness arises by reason
> of intellectual feelings, and in proportion to the variety and
> intensity of such feelings.[55]

The conscious 'feeling' is appended to the last stage of the concrescence and includes all the 'feelings' from the preceding stages.
Here there is general agreement with Bradley, for consciousness
presupposes experience, and not vice versa. For both Whitehead
and Bradley, consciousness is not coextensive with experience.[56]
But clearly Whitehead's discussion of "hybrid" propositional 'feel-

ings' or intellectual 'feelings' would not be acceptable to Bradley's understanding of experience as nonrelational. In Whitehead's view, consciousness illuminates experience, yet it is supported by and contains those more rudimentary phases and subphases of the concrescence. It is the "crown" of experience as a finishing touch. But such occasions that function with this intensity of 'feeling' are highly specialized instances and are few by comparison with those that form moments in the life histories of enduring objects—planets, stones, plants, most animals, etc.

At last, we have come to the completed concrescence where the occasion perishes with respect to its subjective immediacy, and contributes its novel synthesis to the world. Whether the occasion has terminated with the physical purposes, a propositional 'feeling', or in the special instance of an intellectual 'feeling', the result is a satisfaction. The concrescence has built up to a fully determinate entity, and there is a tinge of anticipation that the novel object will have some value beyond the passing moment. As Whitehead puts it, the occasion "really experiences a future which must be actual, although the completed actualities of that future are undetermined. In this sense, each actual occasion experiences its own objective immortality."[57]

By comparison with James or Bradley, Whitehead's theory is excessively complex, especially when we consider all the intricate details of concrescence. It is also rather peculiar that, having gone to such pains to explain epochal becoming as the becoming of undivided unity, he goes on to break down the concrescence with such detail. So it seems to be open to question the sense of the earlier and later phases, or stages, within the concrescence, if, literally, the occasion comes all at once. But for Whitehead we must keep in mind that these stages of growth are not in time and that the analysis of the actual occasion is "only intellectual." He regarded such an analysis as necessary to explain fully the mechanics of process and the possibility of genuine novelty.

Obviously the main point of disagreement between Whitehead and Bradley is whether 'feeling' is intelligible or not, and this depends largely on the interpretation of 'feeling' as relational. Since Bradley regarded 'feeling' as destroyed by a relational interpretation, there was little else he could say other than, analogically speaking, it is a type of unity that gives us some indication of the unity of the Absolute. Whitehead, by contrast, viewed 'feeling' as a type of relation, and therefore regarded it as a component of a much larger experiential process that is open to analysis.

WHITEHEAD'S INTERPRETATION OF BRADLEY

Aside from isolated remarks spread throughout Whitehead's philosophical works, there is one fairly lengthy passage in *Adventures of Ideas* where he has spelled out his indebtedness to Bradley's doctrine of 'feeling'. He says, of course, that there are "grave differences" between his own view and that of Bradley, but he is illustrating here his general adherence to the doctrine and not attempting a detailed analysis of the differences. In this part of our study, however, our purpose will be to understand exactly what these grave differences might come to.

From Bradley's essay on "Immediate Experience" Whitehead quotes:"In my general feeling at any moment there is more than the objects before me, and no perception of objects will exhaust the sense of a living emotion" and says:

> In accordance with this doctrine of Bradley's I analyse a feeling [or prehension] into the 'datum', which is Bradley's 'object before me', into the 'subjective form' which is Bradley's 'living emotion', and into the 'subject' which is Bradley's 'me'.[58]

Furthermore, he goes on in some detail to explain just how he agrees with what he considers to be Bradley's conception of the function of "subjective form" on two interpretations:

> My reason for using the term 'subjective form' is that I stretch its meaning beyond 'emotion'. For example consciousness, if it be present, is an element in the subjective form. This is, of course, a grave divergence from Bradley. Subjective form is the character assumed by the subject by reason of some prehended datum.
>
> But on the whole I conform to Bradley's conception of the function of subjective form. For example, "These puzzles are insoluble unless that which I feel, and which is not an object before me, is present and active. This felt element is used and it

must be used in the constitution of that object which satisfies me".[59]

From my point of view there is an ambiguity in this statement, but I adhere to either alternative meaning.

The component of feeling 'which is not an object before me' is the subjective form. If Bradley is stating that the subjective forms of feelings determine the process of integration, I entirely agree. The result, as Bradley states, is the 'satisfaction' which is the final feeling terminating the unrest of the creative process.

Bradley, however, may mean by this phrase "that which I feel, and which is not an object before me" what I term a "negative prehension." Such a prehension is active *via* its contribution of its subjective form to the creative process, but it dismisses its 'object' from the possibility of entering into the datum of the final satisfaction. This final complex datum will be what Bradley calls "that object that satisfies me." Again I agree.[60]

From this analysis, Whitehead has made it quite clear how his "actual occasion" connects with what we have called Bradley's "momentary finite centre." Surely both agree that 'feeling' sustains any derivative form of existence. And indeed, so long as we are confined to the analysis of any one moment of experience, there is general agreement. This is also suggested by Whitehead's concluding remarks on Bradley's essay when he discusses the unity within an occasion of human experience.[61] But there are several aspects of this analysis that are either discordant with Bradley's doctrine of 'feeling' or altogether unrecognizable

First, for Bradley, 'feeling' is the intuition of Reality beyond the momentary process. It is only when we depart from the general sense of 'feeling' that we are aware of the perpetual shifting of process. For Whitehead, on the other hand, there is a closer alliance between 'feeling' and process. In fact, 'feeling' captures the essence of process and thus functions as the connecting principle whereby the immediate past becomes reenacted in the present occasion. Second, Bradley would have never thought of these statements in such an analytic manner, even though Whitehead does admit that he is stretching the meaning of the terms beyond what Bradley intended. And third, there is some reason to believe that, while Whitehead has captured the gist of Bradley's view, he has pushed Bradley's doctrines much too close to his own, especially when he says that he adheres to either alternative meaning of Bradley's conception of subjective form. In order to understand how this has occurred let us turn to Bradley's essay on "Immediate Experience" for brief exposition.

In this essay, Bradley entertains several thought experiments, some of which are very obscure yet enlightening in terms of defining his concept of 'feeling'. These thought experiments (e.g., attention and introspection) are part of a strategy intended to solve his main problem: How can immediate experience know itself and become for us an object?[62]

In the passages Whitehead has quoted, particularly those in which he finds agreement with his doctrine of subjective form, we find Bradley entangled with the problem of how one can observe what one 'feels' without destroying its felt character. In describing an actual emotion, we objectify it at once, such as when we move from despondency to despondency observed. But with this objectified 'feeling', the whole background of the self from which it was taken does not cease to continue. The self-conscious 'feeling' or objectified emotion that captures our attention does not cancel the felt background from which it was abstracted. As Bradley says: "In order to have an object at all, you must have a felt self before which the object comes."[63] And this whole of the felt self can never be turned into an object. This is what I take Bradley to mean when he says: "These puzzles are insoluble unless that which I feel, and which is not an object before me, is present and active."[64] Immediate experience acts as the whole background of the felt self; it remains at bottom and fundamental, and this is what is "not the object before me." This whole background is much larger than a mere *element* contained in 'feeling'.

It is indeed a curious feature of Bradley's essay that there is an ongoing discussion that does seem fairly close to what Whitehead calls "subjective form." For example, when discussing introspection of the present moment, Bradley says: "the persisting feelings can be felt to jar or to accord with the result of observation."[65] And further:

when I pass psychically from despondency to despondency observed, I have not only a general sense of change to something new, but I feel more specifically the presence or absence of novelty and an agreement or a jar with the object before me.[66]

With this in mind, it is easy to understand how Whitehead finds a affinity with what he calls the "aversion" or "adversion" of the subjective form. In aversion there is some degree of attenuation of the importance of the data, whereas in the adversion, the valuation insures the continued importance of the data. In this regard, it is more likely that Whitehead's first interpretation is closer to Bradley's meaning since the second is ruled out by the fact that, for Bradley, there cannot be anything that is excluded from 'feeling', what Whitehead calls a "negative prehension." But even on the first interpretation there is nothing that gives us any indication of a "satisfaction" in Whitehead's sense of the term, especially when understood as "the final feeling terminating the unrest of the creative process."[67]

When Bradley speaks of "that object which satisfies me," I think he is referring to a type of correspondence between the mood and its description. And this is not the 'satisfaction' in Whitehead's sense of the word—that is, the completion of any particular occasion of experience in its concrescence.

Later in his essay, Bradley finally arrives at the conclusion that immediate experience must seek a higher Reality in which to complete itself. The very fact that it cannot become an object for itself points to something higher. He is thus led to the idea of an object that utterly satisfies, the idea of a complete reality that does not have anything "outside it in the form of an 'elsewhere' or a 'not-yet'."[68] But this is obviously the all-inclusive Reality, the Absolute, which can be the only 'satisfaction' in Bradley's sense of the term. As he says, this idea seems to "meet our demand" and "appears to be the ground on which satisfaction is possible."[69]

It seems fairly obvious that Whitehead has read too much into Bradley's doctrine and has thus overestimated his indebtedness to Bradley. The essay on "Immediate Experience" seems to provide an important point of departure for developing his own position, but as straightforward exegesis of Bradley, it is somewhat inaccurate and misleading. This also seems to be the case with his expression of indebtedness to Locke as having most fully anticipated the main positions of the philosophy of organism. When Whitehead seems to disclose an influence on his doctrines it is much more likely that he wishes to draw an analogy in order to clarify his position.

CHAPTER 4

Internal and External Relations

In the previous chapters we have examined the main principles of Bradley's "infrarelational experience" ('feeling') and to some extent those of the "suprarelational experience" (the Absolute), with respect to affinities and contrasts with Whitehead's metaphysics. We now turn our attention to the relational level of experience which forms a crucial focal point for the present work.

Bradley has made a name for himself in Western philosophic thought for his very rigorous criticism of relations, and for his insistence that the self-contradictory character of relational thought must lead us to the acceptance of a nonrelational Absolute. On the other hand, James and Whitehead have advanced, in their own ways, novel forms of metaphysical pluralism in which concrete relatedness becomes the essential defining characteristic of each actuality in a creative universe. We are thus led to the point where Bradley's challenge must be met.

In this chapter I will expose the thrust of Bradley's arguments against the reality of relations, and then consider various objections and modifications in light of Whitehead's process metaphysics. In the course of evaluating Bradley's arguments, I shall discuss some of the debates between him, James and Russell early in this century. The results of these arguments have become central to the formulation of process thought, implicitly recognized by Whitehead and defended most vigorously in the work of Charles Hartshorne. I shall only occasionally discuss parts of the enormous amount of secondary literature that has been generated by Bradley's arguments in this century. As relevant as much of it may be, it is indeed impossible to deal with it all in one chapter. This, in itself, should indicate the central nerve Bradley has struck in philosophic thinking; for no metaphysics or ontology with any pretensions to adequacy can ignore Bradley's analysis of relations.

BRADLEY ON RELATION AND CONTRADICTION

The problem of relations forms an axis in Bradley's philosophy. It is, in fact, the focus of *Appearance and Reality*, whereby his analysis of philosophic topics thereafter becomes easy game.[1] Once the central thesis of the self-contradictoriness of relations has been established, such themes as time, space, motion, and activity become easy prey for Bradley's dialectic. When we enter the relational level, he insists, we have departed from the relative safety of 'feeling' into a realm of thought and an endless web of terms and relations. The more we affirm the complete independence of objects, the more we fall hopelessly into contradiction and unreality.

Bradley arrives at the theory of relations expounded in "Relation and Quality," chapter III of *Appearance and Reality*, by way of an examination of the distinction between primary and secondary qualities and of the distinction between substantive and adjective. But these two approaches turn out to be unsatisfactory ways of understanding reality, for no real unity can be found existing outside of qualities or within them, and thus the classification of things into properties turns out to be theoretically unintelligible. It is in this connection that Bradley embarks on his discussion of relations and qualities.

In this chapter, Bradley provides four condensed arguments that allegedly encapsulate the subject from all possible perspectives. On this point, Richard Wollheim describes the strategy of this chapter as "pruned to an almost Kantian symmetry of exposition." He writes:

> For each of the two elements [qualities and relations] he seeks to prove, first, that it is impossible without the other, and, secondly, that it is impossible with the other: and he does this first from the side of the terms, then from the side of the relations.[2]

Bradley argues that:

1. Qualities are nothing *without* relations, for qualities are different from one another. "Their plurality depends on relation, and, without that relation, they are not distinct."[3] We cannot even think of a quality without conceiving it as possessing a

character distinct from other qualities. This difference itself implies relation.

2. On the other hand, qualities taken *with* their relations are equally unintelligible. For clearly qualities cannot be reduced to their relations. The qualities must support their relations, and in this sense, they make the relations. But here we are led to a diversity within each quality. As Bradley says: "Each has a double character, as both supporting and as being made by the relation."[4] A quality A has a ground a and a consequent a' of the relation. One is the difference on which distinction is based, while the other is the distinctness that results from their connection. These two aspects are not each the other; nor is either one of them, taken by itself, A. Both are necessary to the constitution of A. But the question arises as to how a and a' are related; and so we are led to postulate a further diversity of grounds and consequents within each, such that a becomes aa and a' becomes $a'a'$ and so on *ad infinitum*. Their seeming solidity is dissipated by what Bradley calls a "principle of fission which conducts us to no end."[5]

3. From the side of relations it is obvious that relations *without* qualities are equally impossible. As Bradley says "a relation without terms seems mere verbiage; and terms appear, therefore, to be something beyond their relation."[6] Something must be related to make the relation, and this something must be the qualities.

4. And finally, if we consider how the relation can stand to the qualities, that is, *with* the qualities, we clearly see that new connecting relations must be introduced to relate the qualities to the original relation. For example, if two qualities A and B are joined by a relation C, a fresh relation D is then required to relate A to C, and so on *ad infinitum*.

The main thrust of these four arguments can be clarified if we take (1) and (3) as directed toward proving that external relations are contradictory and (2) and (4) as directed toward proving that internal relations are also contradictory.

An external relation generally means that the terms of the relation are independent of each other. Bradley, however, has construed the main issue of external relations in terms of the independence of the qualities from the relations, and vice versa. This consideration will engage our attention later in this chapter with regard to various objections to his analysis of the relational complex. Our real concern at the moment is to understand how Bradley derives a contradiction from the analysis of qualities and relations *without* each other—(1) and (3)—and how the other two arguments—(2) and (4)—are logically dependent upon this conclusion.

Taken from either side, qualities and relations are clearly impossible without each other. Obviously any attempt to arrive at a quality without a relation (1) or a relation without qualities (3) is doomed to failure. Even in complete abstraction this remains a conceptual impossibility. In argument (1), which amounts to the same thing as (3) from the other side, the contradiction arises as a result of the two clashing points: If two qualities are different from each other, there must be something outside of them that accounts for their difference; however, if what accounts for this difference simply falls between the two qualities, then the qualities can be conceived without the relation. External relations, then, cannot be real because they must fall between their terms and, at the same time, form part of their terms.

Now that the failure of the mutual independence between qualities and relations has been established, the next two arguments—(2) and (4)—are advanced on the basis of this conclusion. Since qualities and relations cannot be independent, they must be dependent and therefore internally related. But still they prove to be contradictory for Bradley. These two arguments are both characterized by an infinite regress; one within any one particular quality in the relation, and the other between any one quality and the original connecting relation. The main point here is that a contradiction inherent in the very idea of an internal relation gives rise to a vicious infinite regress.

Since an internal relation implies that the terms of the relation cannot be conceived apart from it, (2), a quality implies the existence of something distinct from the relation which at the same time forms part of the relation. This creates an internal division within each quality such that each divides into two elements that are conceivable apart from the relation. This new division means that the terms of internal relations consist of parts that are externally related to each other, and this process of division is infinite because we can now keep generating new content of subterms and subrelations *ad infinitum*. So internal relations cannot be real because such relations both are, and are not, distinct from their terms. From the other side, (4), the conception of a relation in this situation cannot be a mere adjective of the qualities, and being something substantial, it cannot accomplish the necessary linking. As Bradley emphasizes: "If you take the connection as a solid thing, you have got to show, and you cannot show, how the other solids are joined to it." [7] Other links must be therefore introduced between the connection, and this ends up in a hopeless web of relations of relations, and so on. Here internal relations cannot possibly be real because they simply do not relate. One solid thing, the relation, does not link another solid thing, the quality. The relation cannot be nothing, yet it cannot be something.

Hence, for Bradley, both external and internal relations are contradictory and therefore can not possibly characterize ultimate reality. As he himself says in a later essay:

> To take reality as a relational scheme, no matter whether the relations are 'external' or 'internal', seems therefore impossible and perhaps even ridiculous. It would cease to be so only if the immediacy of feeling could be shown to be merely relational.[8]

With this, however, there is a certain qualification of Bradley's doctrine regarding the status of internal relations. We may distinguish in his thought a level of experience between the relational level and the suprarelational level (i.e., the Absolute) where all relations are internal. On the strata of degrees of truth and reality, internal relations more closely represent reality as One, rather than many, and are therefore to be considered more real. At least we are here moving away from the extreme pluralist thesis of a universe of self-contained individuals to a view that emphasizes mutual dependence. And indeed, for Bradley, relations do exist and, in some sense, qualify the Absolute, but in a distorted way; internal ones distorting it less than external ones.[9]

Finally, to complete this section, it should be clear that the four arguments of *Appearance and Reality* focus on a general empiricist outlook. The relational complex (i.e., the arrangement of qualities and the connecting relation) is an abstraction from any one moment of experience that comes before the mind as a complex impression. For instance, when one considers the relation between two shades of blue, one might be abstracting a relational complex from a variety of books on a shelf. But even though Bradley's arguments here are primarily concerned with a type of spatial relatedness, it is quite clear that he intends their application to all forms of terms and relations. For example, in *The Principles of Logic*, he uses the same approach with regard to units of 'feeling' and their temporal relations.[10] This is central to our present analysis, for we shall focus attention on the movement between discrete moments of experience and their temporal order. In any case, whatever way the arguments are applied, Bradley's contention is that *any* form of relatedness always presupposes, and is therefore dependent upon, an underlying unity.[11] They are at best an invention of thought, useful for our practical understanding, but never considered fully real.

CONCRETE RELATEDNESS AND PREHENSION

In one way or another Bradley, James, and Whitehead all agree upon the central place of immediate experience or 'feeling' in their respective metaphysical systems. Bradley's "finite centres of experience," James's "drops of experience" and Whitehead's "actual occasions" all point to the same concrete facts of immediate 'feeling'. However the rationality inherent in this flow of experience takes on radically different interpretations in the monist and pluralist versions. In one sense, all agree that the intellect harms our intuitive grasp of reality. James, for example, argues that the intellect can only deal with a type of retrospective "patchwork" or "post-mortem dissection" since it cannot keep pace with the cutting edge of immediacy. For Whitehead, the problem centers on language and the difficulties of expressing this dynamic flow of reality in terms of the static subject-predicate form of proposition. And for Bradley, the leap into the relational level of thought always distorts that continuous whole present in 'feeling'. The main point seen by each is a certain injustice done to concrete experience once analysis has cut into what is essentially alive and harmonious. But with the various attempts of these thinkers to construct a system from this basis, Bradley has denied that the flow of experience can be made up of genuine individuals and their relations. The main challenge from the side of pluralism, then, is to show that relations are contained in immediate feeling. Bradley saw this himself when he said that the unreality of relations "would cease to be so only if the immediacy of feeling could be shown to be merely relational."[12] This is exactly the point of James's objections to Bradley, in which he sought to expose the sophistical features of the arguments, what he called the "intellectualist logic" of absolute idealism; it is also the main focus of Whitehead's modification of the Bradleian concept of feeling.

Before we move on to James's objections, let us consider what has been established by Bradley's antirelational arguments. Surely an extreme pluralism of self-contained, self-sufficient individuals and purely external relations would be contradictory. In this regard, Bradley's arguments (1) and (3) are effective in showing the absurdity of terms without relations and relations without terms. The relations and the terms must be more intimate, and in some sense dependent upon each other. The terms must involve the relation, and the relation must involve the terms.

The very roots of this problem are to be found in the Cartesian definition of substance as "that which requires nothing but itself in order to exist" rigorously applied to each of Hume's clear and distinct impressions of sensation. Hume, in fact, recognized the problem of relations when he asked: "What is the necessary connection between distinct impressions?"; but he came to the very opposite conclusion from Bradley when he defended their separate existence.[13] But individual independence construed in this way does make the problem of relations a "metaphysical nuisance." Two terms and an abstract universal, the relation, simply do not accomplish the necessary linking. What is therefore required to explain the continuity of experience is a type of penetration and possession by the terms, and in this sense, pluralism must make certain concessions to Bradley.

As early as *The Concept of Nature*, Whitehead expressed his doubts about the doctrine of external relations and its ability to account for the system of nature. As he put it:

The false idea we have to get rid of is that of nature as a mere aggregate of independent entities, each capable of isolation. According to this conception these entities, whose characteristics are capable of isolated definition, come together and by their accidental relations form the system of nature. . . .

The explanation of nature which I urge as an alternative ideal to this accidental view of nature, is that nothing in nature could be what it is except as an ingredient in nature as it is.[14]

It is on this score that Whitehead begins his appeal to a more Bradleian type of thought, eventually issuing in a metaphysics that includes both internal and external relations.

Standing between the radical pluralism of Hume and Russell and the radical monism of Spinoza and Bradley, James and Whitehead have both defended what James has called "the legitimacy of the notion of some," for, as James argued: "each part of the world is in some ways connected, in some other ways not connected with its other parts, and the ways can be discriminated."[15] James sought some mediated course between the two extremes: absolute independence and absolute mutual dependence. This mediated position provides for a synthesis of rationalism and empiricism. In advancing this position, he asks:

May not the flux of sensible experience itself contain a rationality that has been overlooked, so that the real remedy would consist in harking back to it more intelligently, and not in advancing in the opposite direction away from it . . .?[16]

The real question is how the things of this world can have any connection among one another without denying that they exist in their own right.

Unlike Bradley, James begins with the parts, with the individual drops of experience, and then arrives at conjunctive relations through the continuity between these penetrating moments. James therefore insists, contrary to Bradley, that these relations are experienced as continuity. For him, the Absolute is unnecessary to explain the connection of things. It is a being of the second order resulting from the over-intellectualist tendencies of transcendentalism.

For James the problem of internal and external relations is reformulated as "conjunctive" and "disjunctive" relations. Conjunctive relations are those that are perceived as continuity within the stream of experience; each drop interpenetrates among the other members of one stream or another to form a continuum. Taken in this manner, a conjunctive relation is our most basic sense of the past flowing onward into the immediate present. Disjunctive relations, on the other hand, are experiences of separation or of mere *with-ness* such as experiences of disunion felt when breaks are made from a thing lived to another thing only conceived.[17] The sense of separateness of streams provides for a genuine plurality of individuals. For James, the world is a collection where some parts of experience are conjoined and others disjoined, even though the disjoined parts may nonetheless hang together by intermediaries that are conjoined. Thus instead of absolute unity or absolute disunity, James contends that the world is a *concatenated* unity so long as *some* path of conjunction is available between disjoined parts.[18]

According to this account, both disjunctive and conjunctive relations are just as real as the terms that they relate.[19] In an appeal to the reality of relations of every type, James argues that:

> Every examiner of the sensible life *in concreto* must see that relations of every sort, of time, space, difference, likeness, change, rate, cause, or what not, are just as integral members of sensational flux as terms are, and that conjunctive are just as true members of the flux as disjunctive relations are.[20]

In the process of time, innumerable individual terms become and are superseded by others which follow upon them by transition of both conjunctive and disjunctive content. And these relations themselves, being integral components of the process, must be accounted as at least as real as the terms.

As far as James's analysis is concerned, he seems to have a difficulty accounting for the relations between the terms. That is, within the vibrant flow of experience, the relation and the matter related are indistinguishable. All seems to melt together. Moreover, there seems to be another difficulty in his thinking that does not meet Bradley's objection. If relations are fully co-ordinate parts of experience, they are substantial entities, and one still has to show how they do the job of relating. But these problems can be solved by the sense in which we understand the relation's function in experience, and it is in Whitehead that we eventually find a more satisfactory account.

Bradley, of course, rejected James's account of conjunctive and disjunctive relations on the grounds that such distinctions are merely abstract constructions and cannot possibly belong to immediate experience.[21] He argued that our first awareness of temporal and spatial diversity is not experienced as having a relational form but rather as a fluid whole. For him, relations are distinguished at the level of conceptual activity. But for James, Bradley has simply muddled the relation between the conceptual form and the perceptual form instead of showing how they supplement each other.[22] The relational form is simply an integral part of immediate feeling.

James argues that continuity itself is a definite sort of experience. We feel the difference between two distinct emotions and we feel the transition as one continues into the other. As he put the point in his *Psychology*: "the *feeling* of the thunder is also a feeling of the silence as just gone." [23] The immanence of one moment in the next is continuity and relatedness.

For James, the mistake in the anti-relational arguments lies in Bradley's understanding of the relation as a purely "external go-between." In several places he attacks Bradley's argument (4) as a prime example of what he calls a "vertiginous *regressus ad infinitum*." [24] Instead of taking conjunctive relations at face value, Bradley asks for some ineffable union in the abstract: How does a relation relate? But clearly this approach is bound to lead to contradiction. Instead of hooking A to B, and bridging the original chasm, the relation C itself requires another hook to bridge the second chasm created by this process, and so on *ad infinitum*. But taken in this way, a relation is nothing more than an abstraction from the concrete relatedness of moments in time.

Many who have opposed Bradley have failed to refute his arguments because they have made their objections within the same abstract context in which he set up the problems. For example, many of McTaggart's and Russell's arguments fall into this category.[25] James and Whitehead, however, are more effective critics of Bradley because they approach the problem of relations within the context of immediate experience.

Of the many influences on Whitehead's concept of the actual occasion, James must certainly be mentioned for elucidating the basic psychological groundwork for the metaphysical principle. Moreover, the basic concept of prehension underlying an occasion's grasp of its immediate past bears a remarkable affinity to the Jamesian concept of conjunctive relations and the view that life exists in the transitions. For Whitehead, as for James, Bradley's infrarelational and relational levels of experience are collapsed into one level of process. Here the rationality discerned in immediate experience provides understanding instead of contradictions.

Both James and Whitehead appeal to the simplicity of the "plain conjunctive experience" in their attempt to understand the linkage of moments in the passage of time. It is here that a crucial distinction arises regarding two very different types of relations: one concrete sense in which they are parts of the terms and another abstract sense in which they are seen as universals or logical connectives. With James we have seen that a relation C cannot be a purely "external go-between" in accomplishing the linkage of two moments A and B. That is, it cannot be seen as a distinct entity separate from the moments to be related. If this was so, the relation simply would not be experienced as part of the flow. Anything in between or outside of the primary experiential units must therefore be given up as an abstraction. On this point, the objection to Bradley runs fairly close to one of the better points made by Russell when he said: "Bradley conceives a relation as something just as substantial as its terms, and not radically different in kind." [26] James, of course, never put the point in quite this way, but a certain reading of him tends in this direction. Victor Lowe, for example, in a paper entitled "William James and Whitehead's Doctrine of Prehensions," has made a somewhat similar point by reformulating James's view that "The parts of experience hold together from next to next *by relations that are themselves parts of experience*," to mean, "The drops of experience hold together from next to next by transitions that are felt as components contributing to the drops of experience." [27] Relations are not themselves entities of some extraexperiential type, but rather aspects of the drops that do the connecting. They are parts of the internal mechanism of process. Whitehead argued this when he said something to the effect that: There is no objection to the purely logical use of the term *relation*. Relations are universals such as *between, believing,* and *greater than.* In this sense the connectedness of occasions may be said to exemplify an abstract universal, but such connection is not itself a universal; it is a "real particular fact" in the history of the world.[28] Prehension and felt transmission are therefore better understood as the real connection of things, though the term *relation* is often used in a generic sense to cover both the abstract and concrete.

The line of thought that emphasizes the reality of the individuals and their concrete relations is characteristic of much of the new realism that reacted against absolute idealism at the outset of this century. When Bradley says that a relation cannot account for the fact of relatedness, he is confusing the abstract universal with the concrete connection of things. That is, in conceiving terms and relations, he gives the relation the same ontological status that he gives the terms. Bradley emphasizes in several places that a relation exists only "between" terms.[29] He asks: "If relations are facts that exist *between* facts, then what comes *between* the relations and the other facts?"[30] And elsewhere he says: "Take a relational situation and examine it. You cannot say that the terms are the relation, or the relation is the terms."[31] But what he misses is the idea that the terms themselves can involve relatedness as an essential defining characteristic.[32]

In Whitehead's ontology the actual occasion is the concrete unit of experience. Its essential defining characteristic is its prehension of past actualities. Whitehead therefore avoids the notion of an ontological entity in the form of a relation that comes between actual occasions. There is nothing between actual occasions but other actual occasions. Relations between are nothing more than a derivative abstraction from the concrete process. Thus, logically speaking, *aRb* is read "the relation of *a* to *b*" not "*a* in relation to *R* in relation to *b.*"

Given the above argument, it is clear that Bradley's analysis of the relational complex is flawed, and as a consequence, his argument (4) is refuted by rejecting the abstract relation. At this point, however, we have not addressed the problems raised by his argument (2) in which an infinite regress occurs within each term.

Having done away with the unnecessary entity, the relation, the argument could still hold when we consider the difference between two related terms. As we recall, Bradley's argument was that by being in relationship, *A* is not simply what it is, but what it is as related to *B*. *A*, then, is both the ground and the consequent of the relationship, which raises the problem of the relationship between *A* as ground *a*, and *A* as consequent *a'*, and so on.

Though Whitehead has not explicitly referred to the problems raised by this argument, his solution can be found in the doctrine of becoming and perishing—the double character of temporal passage. In the case of two occasions *A* and *B* related by their contiguous temporal order, *A* must be understood as having perished with regard to its subjective immediacy even though it does exist as an object to be prehended by the initial stage of *B*'s becoming. But here too much emphasis on the succession of discrete moments can create insurmountable problems for the prehension of the past. [33] In other words, how can a present occasion prehend what is no longer there? What occurs in this transition must therefore be much more fluid and moving. At the end point of *A*'s satisfaction, it merges into a passive (conformal) stage of *B*. As *A* perishes, it becomes part of a future concrescing occasion. But "perishing" in this sense does not mean that it disappears. On the contrary, it is at this point that *A* appears as a determinate entity and becomes available to the initial prehensions of *B*. It should therefore be clear that, in this temporal sequence, *B* is not determinate in the same sense as *A*. That is, *A* and *B* are not simultaneously existent but rather the preceding occasion has perished as 'subject' while its superject has merged into the novel becoming of the successor (and all other occasions in the future that will prehend its objects).

With this in mind, Whitehead must agree with Bradley that each occasion is both ground and consequent, cause and effect of relationship; but this does not involve an infinite regress within each occasion. The fact that the occasions perish prevents their internal fission.

The doctrine of the subject-superject means that each actual occasion is a conditioned subject becoming effect. It arises out of

decisions already made in the antecedent world, and it determines the possibilities for its successors. As Whitehead says: "The
cause is objectively in the constitution of the effect, in virtue of
being the feeler of the feeling reproduced in the effect with partial
equivalence of subjective form."[34] But the passage of occasions in
time differentiates their representation as a mere line of self-
contained entities.

Bradley, of course, understands quite well that a world of
finite entities would mean that the entities either hang together by
threads from the past or perish internally in a vanishing network
of neverending relations.[35] But what he failed to consider was
how the moments of experience themselves could be contained in
one another. In *Appearance and Reality*, he says, for example,
that so far as we know, finite centres of feeling, while they last,
are not directly pervious to one another.[36] But this consideration
was not crucial for him since the Absolute provides the basis for
their unity. Whitehead, on the other hand, has articulated the
ground for unity in the universe by the prehensions in each occasion. One occasion of experience is not simply related to another
by airy threads. It is, rather, immanent in that occasion, if it
occurred in its past. This is what Whitehead meant when he said
that his actual occasion constitutes an inversion of Bradley's doctrine of actuality.[37] Each occasion contains elements of the whole
of past history just as, for Bradley, the Absolute contains everything in one single Experience.

Insofar as Whitehead has given a new temporal meaning to
the many-into-one concept, certain qualifications must be made.
Each occasion is determined by its own unique subjective aim
and thereby forms a new synthesis of its relations to the immediate past world. This involves selection and elimination in order
that the exact degree in which the present moment contains the
past can be determined. Each occasion is present in every other,
but only in a transmuted and partial sense. Thus, as Whitehead
argues, "if we allow for degrees of relevance, and for negligible
relevance, we must say that every actual entity is present in every
other actual entity."[38] This, however, does not include contemporaries or successors. At the moment in which the occasion becomes, its immediate predecessors are the only actualities that are

there to be included in the initial stage of its concrescence, and these occasions include bits of the whole of cosmic history.

SYMMETRICAL AND ASYMMETRICAL RELATIONS

One of the most serious objections to Bradley's notion of an all-inclusive Absolute is the inability of the theory to deal adequately with the problems raised by the fact of asymmetrical relations. Russell and the proponents of the new realism were first to formulate this criticism against Bradley, and much of this strand of thought has continued into process philosophy, though with considerable modification.

Unlike Moore, who focused his attention on the refutation of idealism, Russell was preoccupied with the refutation of monism. He argued that monism could not accommodate the types of asymmetrical relations that are fundamental to various aspects of reality. At the heart of the matter, Russell attacked what he called the doctrine of internal relations—that each part of reality has a nature which exhibits its relations to every other part and to the whole.[39] He linked this doctrine with both the monadistic theory of Leibniz—that a relation between two terms is a property of them, and the monistic theory of Bradley—that every relation implies a property of an inclusive whole.[40] But leaving Leibniz aside, let us concentrate our attention on his objections to Bradley.

One of the most important grounds that Russell advanced against the monistic theory of relations is the difference of order that occurs in asymmetrical relations, and this means that at least some relations must be external. An asymmetrical relation aRb, Russell says, implies a unique irreversible order. How can a whole that includes such a relation account for the uniqueness, say, in a's being larger than b? In such a situation there exists an irreversibility of order and a distinction of sense that raises a difficulty for a monistic theory of relations. Even if we say, with Bradley, that in the Absolute, the relation $(ab)r$ contains diversity of magnitude, the question still remains as to whether "a is larger than b" or "b is larger than a."

Russell also argues that the monistic theory fails to explain relations between whole and part that are necessarily asymmetrical in nature. If, for example, we take the proposition "*a* is a part of *b*," the monistic theory cannot distinguish between the whole composed of *(ab)* and the whole *b* which contains *a* as one of its parts. As Russell says, if we regard the proposition about the new whole to be one that does not concern whole and part, then "there will be no true judgments of whole and part, and it will therefore be false to say that a relation between the parts is really an adjective of the whole."[41] On the other hand, if the proposition does say something about whole-part relations, we find ourselves in an infinite regress in which the proposition always presupposes another whole.

Such criticisms were crucial to Russell's early work where he was concerned largely with the foundations of mathematics. His contention was that, until his time, inadequate or incorrect theories of relations hindered both the development of logic and philosophy in general, and that the ground cleared in *The Principles of Mathematics* would give new direction and impetus to these fields of study. The problem with the monistic and monadistic theories is that they made mathematics inexplicable. But external relations and specifically those of an asymmetrical sort are essential to a theory of mathematics where we must be able to make distinctions of order and sense for quantitative differences. The real question for Russell, however, concerns the extent to which such relations serve as a basis for metaphysics.

Bradley's replies to these objections are contained in a few sketchy and incomplete notes appended to the posthumous essay, "Relations." But even though he did not specifically address the two problems raised by Russell, he did offer a general reply that no relations can possibly be ultimate, asymmetrical or otherwise. First, as we have emphasized above, Bradley never admitted any sort of genuine individuals and their relations into 'feeling.' His continuous Absolute cannot therefore be understood as individuated into self-subsistent parts. No whole is really a simple whole. This is why the attempt to predicate qualities of the whole falls short of Reality.[42] Second, Bradley argues that there is a definite difference between the unity present in 'feeling' and mere asymmetrical relations. "Feeling," he says, "contains everything, which clearly asymmetrical relations do not."[43] It is, in this sense, nonrelational and directionless. And third, whatever is distinguished at the relational level of experience cannot be understood as representative of the Absolute. Bradley admits that there are these two classes of relations, symmetrical and asymmetrical, and that order and direction are involved in the latter. But since relations clash with the given unity of 'feeling', they are always an abstraction from our actual experience and must be grounded in a wider whole. Once again, they may serve our practical understanding (e.g., larger-smaller, whole-part, before-after), but they distort our conception of reality if taken as ultimate.

Thus, Bradley defends his monism against the charge of asymmetrical relations only by invoking his notion of levels of experience, in which distinctions are made at the relational level of perception and thought but do not hold true at the infrarelational and the suprarelational levels. However, since we have clearly rejected these levels of experience as artificially contrived, much of this line of argument falls apart. The concrete relatedness that we experience from one moment to the next is identical to 'feeling' in the general sense. Once this is realized, the great mystery in Bradley's theory vanishes.

The Russell-Bradley problem, put in a certain way, asks: Are relations external or internal to their terms?[44] If there are many "reals" and they are purely internally related, there can be no real independence between them. On the other hand, if they are purely externally related, there can be no real togetherness and dependence of things. Either side taken to its extreme leads to incoherence. But what is overlooked in this dilemma is the possibility of internal-external relations, dependence-independence taken together. Bradley says: "Pluralism, to be consistent, must, I presume, accept the reality of external relations."[45] But granted the necessity of this point, does the admission of external relations exclude the possibility of internal relations? In fact, internal and external relations require each other if either is not to collapse into meaninglessness, or with Bradley, into unreality.[46]

Whitehead and Hartshorne have synthesized the seemingly opposed doctrines into a persuasive and coherent scheme of process. The novel formulation of this view belongs to Whitehead, even though it has been strengthened by the very clarity with which Hartshorne has stated and defended the position.[47] The most fundamental thesis of their new doctrine, "event-pluralism," is that the universe evolves by an asymmetric process of causality in which former actualities are prehended by latter ones, but not vice versa. The temporal order of occasions via causal prehensions provides a genuine directedness of experience where dependence is conceived as one-way; an actual occasion of the immediate present is dependent on those of the past, having prehended the objects for its novel synthesis, but a past occasion is not dependent upon those of the present. That is, a previous actual occasion, having perished, cannot prehend the present and is therefore not dependent upon what follows its completed synthesis.

Given a simple nexus of causal prehensions,

$$A \to B \to C \to D$$

where D represents an immediate present occasion and A, B, and C represent past occasions, an immediate past occasion C is internally related to D, having contributed its datum to the creative choice in the future, but is externally related to A and B in its past. D must therefore be conceived as dependent upon A, B, and C in its past, but A, B, and C are independent of D, which occurs in their future. In this sequence, C could not have prehended what, in its subjective immediacy, did not exist, namely, the occasion D. But D, arising into existence through causation is the accumulation of the process by its positive prehensions of C and all other occasions that were contemporaries of C, i.e., the multitude of occasions that were becoming at the same time as C. The elements that were negatively prehended by D were eliminated, yet they remain relevant by the fact that they were considered in the final determination. These negative prehensions would most probably have been prehended positively by the many contemporaries of D.

Contemporary occasions (i.e., occasions that do not occur in the past or future of the subject in question) happen in causal independence of one another. Since an immediately concrescing subject can only prehend what is in its immediate past, its contemporaries are still immersed in the genetic process and are therefore unavailable. An actual occasion becomes public only when its private self-creation is completed. This contemporaneity and causal independence of the present is the ground for pluralism and freedom in the world. Contemporary occasions in the immediate present cannot prehend one another in a symmetrical relationship. Whitehead, for example, writes: "It is the definition of contemporary events that they happen in causal independence of each other. Thus two contemporary occasions are such that neither belongs to the past of the other."[48] There is, however, for Whitehead, an indirect sense in which contemporaries may be connected:

> The mutual independence of contemporary occasions lies strictly within the sphere of their teleological self-creation. The occasions originate from a common past and their objective immortality operates within a common future. Thus indirectly, *via* the immanence of the past and the immanence of the future, the occasions are connected. But the immediate activity of self-creation is separate and private, so far as contemporaries are concerned.[49]

Contemporaries, then, are indirectly immanent with regard to their prehensions of a common past, which is a common overlapping of their causal antecedents and the extension beyond to the anticipation of their causal consequents. In the overlap of the actual world of two contemporaries *A* and *B*, both prehend a third occasion *C* (or nexus of occasions) in the antecedent environment. This makes *C* common to *A* and *B*, and provides a ground for an indirect immanence of *A* in *B*, and *B* in *A*. That is, they share in a common immediacy by prehending the same datum, and are therefore in a unison of becoming. Also, a fourth occasion *D* in the immediate future will prehend the objects of *A* and *B*, and thereby provide a further ground for their immanence.

The result of this analysis is that actual occasions are internally related at one end and externally related at the other. This substantially modifies the Jamesian doctrine of conjunctive-disjunctive relations discussed in the last section. Whitehead holds that the internal-external dichotomy is not simply one in which internal relations occur only within any one stream of experience while external ones occur as a result of a break within or without the stream. Rather, internal and external relations are grounded in the temporal asymmetry of process where, at each successive moment, the world moves from disjunctive diversity to conjunctive unity. However in accordance with the Jamesian spirit of the world connected in some ways and not connected in others, process philosophy steers a mediated course between two extremes: radical pluralism and radical monism, to formulate what Hartshorne has called, in opposition to new realism, the "New Idealism" or "realistic Idealism." This new doctrine also develops the concept of asymmetry well beyond the type of problems Russell advanced against Bradley.

From Hartshorne's analysis of the principles of symmetry and asymmetry contained in previous philosophical thought, he argues that regardless of such issues that divide one from another (idealism, realism, monism, pluralism), the "fallacy of misplaced symmetry" has prejudiced our ability to see reality as directional and open at one end.[50] Bradley, Russell, and Hume, for example, all fall into the fallacy of assuming symmetry in what is essentially one-way. Bradley's antirelational arguments assume that, given two terms, they are either mutually interdependent or mutually independent. Both Russell and Hume, on the other hand, accept the same starting point, but prefer the radically pluralistic alternative of disconnected terms.[51] On the one hand *external*, has always meant external to both terms, and complete independence, while *internal* has meant holding at both ends, and complete mutual dependence. As we saw in the first section of this chapter, this was exactly the context in which Bradley argued for the unreality of both external and internal relations. Arguments (1) and (3) assumed mutual independence, while arguments (2) and (4) assumed mutual dependence. The whole formulation of the problem assumed symmetry. Russell, on the other side, used the asymmetrical case against Bradley but only from the point of view of the external relations. He missed the importance of the temporal aspect of reality central to the correct formulation of the internal-external, dependence-independence dichotomy, and he therefore failed to generalize his objection that the asymmetrical case had been neglected.

According to Hartshorne, the symmetrical fallacy is so deeply ingrained in philosophical thinking that even those who accept the asymmetrical principle as fundamental, unconsciously fall into a language which assumes symmetry. James and Bergson speak of the flow of reality as "interpenetrating" or "melting together." Whitehead often says that his actual occasions are "interdependent." But the prefix *inter-*, which suggests both-way influence, is inconsistent with the idea of occasions penetrating one-way. Nature is an ocean of 'feelings', but the crucial qualification on this idea is that the 'feelings' in nature that are given to our experiences are independent of those experiences.

EXTENSIVE RELATIONS AND ABSTRACTION

Thus far the discussion of the Whiteheadian view of relations has been simplified in order to clarify the exact points of disagreement with Bradley. The concrete relatedness of actual occasions, however, does not cover the entire spectrum of Whitehead's ontology. Aside from the concrete facts of experience—actual occasions, prehensions and nexūs—Whitehead derives by abstraction other types of entities—eternal objects, propositions, multiplicities, contrasts, and a hierarchy of societies—that form the full complexity of his cosmological structure. Our task here is to reveal some of the complexity of his theory by an analysis of the extensive relations discerned in the perceptive mode of presentational immediacy. This brings us to Whitehead's idea of an "extensive continuum" as one ultimate relational scheme that underlies the process of actual occasions. Then we examine another relational scheme of pure abstraction, the realm of eternal objects.

Unlike Bradley, Whitehead's previous concerns with mathematics, projective and descriptive geometry became essential to the construction of his metaphysics and his cosmology. Systems of relations were therefore crucial to Whitehead's whole project, and this becomes clear in both his attempts to construct a theory of extension and a theory of universals. Part IV of *Process and Reality* is concerned with developing a complex relational scheme of extension which for him provides the basis for any scientific analysis and measurement. The theory of universals, on the other hand, is mainly developed in the chapter on abstraction in *Sci-*

ence and the Modern World and concerns the relatedness of pure potentials.

As we recall from chapter 2, presentational immediacy is the mode of perception in which the contemporary world presents itself as clear and distinct extensive relations of time, space and sensa. From causal efficacy, sensa are inherited and projected onto the presented locus as eternal objects belonging to the occasions that make up the contemporary world. This is our ordinary sense of perception where objects are perceived as having various properties. But clearly we do not directly perceive the contemporary world as a multitude of atomic occasions. Rather we perceive a group of entities acting as a unity; the nexus is objectified and its constitution is illustrated by extensive relationships with ingredient eternal objects that discriminate parts of the extensive region.

Within the presented locus, the contemporary world is divisible into various subregions that are themselves contemporaries. We are aware of geometrical relations that define the regions and make up the structures of extended space-time. But beyond these geometrical relations, Whitehead contends there are more general relations of extensive connection that are nonmetrical and topological and form the most general aspects of an extensive continuum. This fundamental scheme of relations is, in fact, a metaphysical assumption for his account of presentational immediacy.

According to Whitehead, as the universe evolves and actuality continually weaves itself among the patterns of possibility, it is in virtue of one ultimate system that intellectual comprehension of the physical universe is possible.[52] All actualities are related to one another according to determinations of "one basic scheme of extensive connection which expresses on one uniform plan (i) the general conditions to which the bonds, uniting the atomic actualities into a nexus, conform, and (ii) the general conditions to which the bonds, uniting the infinite number of coordinate subdivisions of the satisfaction of any actual entity, conform."[53] As occasions become objectified, the extensive scheme takes on the dual aspect of both external and internal relations. With regard to (i), extensive relationships must be conceived as external since these are the bonds between divided things; and with regard to (ii), the solidarity of the physical world arises out of relationships that must be internal to the individual actualities.[54] There are in this way extensive relations *between* things and extensive relations *in* things.

We must bear in mind for the moment that the extensive scheme of relations is an abstraction from the creative process of occasions. So the internal and external relations that apply here do not concern the asymmetry of the creative process, but rather the extensive scheme that arises out of this process. In presentational immediacy, we perceive an extensive continuum that is a potential for division; and since the entities that make up the regions of our contemporary world are causally independent, we find that the objective content of these entities forms external relations. These external relations must, at the same time, be conceived as internal to the actual occasions that make up the extensive scheme.

Whitehead defines the continuum in one particularly clear passage:

> This extensive continuum is one relational complex in which all potential objectifications find their niche. It underlies the whole world, past, present, and future. Considered in its full generality, apart from the additional conditions proper only to the cosmic epoch of electrons, protons, molecules, and star systems, the properties of this continuum are very few and do not include the relationships of metrical geometry. An extensive continuum is a complex of entities united by the various allied relationships of whole to part, and of overlapping so as to possess common parts, and of contact, and of other relationships derived from these primary relationships. The notion of a 'continuum' involves both the property of indefinite divisibility and the property of unbounded extension. There are always entities beyond entities, because nonentity is no boundary. This extensive continuum expresses the solidarity of all possible standpoints throughout the whole process of the world.[55]

The continuum can be conceived in two principal ways: (i) in terms of social order increasing until finally we arrive at the most general form of social relatedness, "pure extension," and (ii) in terms of "real potentiality." In this section we are concerned with real potentiality, though our discussion presupposes the notion of a society constituted by the most general sort of order, namely "pure extensiveness." The extensive continuum, from the point of view of increasing social order, will be discussed in the following chapter on the theory of society and cosmic epochs.

From the point of view of real potentiality, then, the continuum is an abstract structure, "one relational complex," that provides the most general limitation upon actuality. Every actual occasion will exhibit the features of extensive connection. Such features, Whitehead says, are probably metaphysically ultimate and operate in any cosmic epoch of physical occasions. The extensive continuum therefore provides the first and most general order in metaphysics. But it should be clear that the continuum "is not a fact prior to the world; it is the first determination of order—that is, of real potentiality—arising out of the general character of the world." [56] As real potential, it reveals the general conditions for all becoming, and this includes actual occasions and cosmic epochs that may never become actualized.

Since actual occasions atomize the continuum, they make real what was antecedently merely potential. With the becoming of each occasion, there is the production of a certain quantum of extensiveness, of physical time and physical space. But the novel occasion must conform to the past, and this past includes such general features of extensive order. This is why Whitehead says that the extensive continuum underlies the whole world, past, present, and future. Each occasion, regardless of its more special characteristics, must be systematically related according to the general properties of whole and part, overlapping, contact, and various other types of geometrical order that make up the stability of the world. The potential becomes actual as occasions in the future form a bond with the structure in the already settled past.

This purely extensive sort of order also limits the genuine possibilities of the realm of eternal objects since real potentiality constitutes a limitation on abstract possibility. That is, the extensive continuum determines which of the eternal objects are real as opposed to pure possibilities. In the contemporary world we discern clear-cut definitions of sensa, located in definite spatial regions. These are the eternal objects that have become real possibilities by the fact that they were compatible with the requirements of this special sort of order in the immediate past. On this point, Whitehead writes: "The actual entity is the product of the interplay of physical pole with mental pole. In this way, potentiality passes into actuality, and extensive relations mould qualitative content and objectifications of other particulars into a coherent finite experience."[57]

Eternal objects are forms of definiteness. They are endless in variety and include those of an objective species such as mathematical and geometrical forms, and those of a subjective species such as colors, sounds, belief-characters, and emotions. Other types include patterns, relations (as abstractions from contrasts), and grades of generic abstraction. Eternal objects are virtually anything definite that we recognize in the concrete process again and again.

Whitehead does not attempt an exhaustive classification of eternal objects nor does he explain in any detail how the different types are related to one another. Indeed, in *Process and Reality* he does not even speak of a realm of eternal objects but only of a "multiplicity." But in *Science and the Modern World* he explains how eternal objects are related to the concrete process and how those of a particular type are related in a complex hierarchy of grades.

As real possibilities, eternal objects of the objective species ingress into the objective datum of the occasion, while those of the subjective species ingress into the objective datum and the subjective form of the occasion. The concept of ingression expresses the relationship of eternal objects to the actual occasions. It is the particular mode in which the potentiality of an eternal object is realized in a particular occasion. This relationship involves the principle of asymmetry in that the relationship between an eternal object A and an actual occasion a is external as regards A and is internal as regards a.[58] So with regard to the relation between potentiality and actuality, there is an indeterminateness that expresses the eternal object's "indifferent patience for any mode of ingression into any actual occasion."[59] Potentiality is indifferent to actuality; and such indeterminateness is necessary for external relations. But from the standpoint of the occasion, there is a determinate relatedness that expresses the mode of realization of the eternal objects for that occasion, and these relations are therefore internal.

But now quite apart from the concrete process of actual occasions and the real possibilities that characterize the constituent occasions, eternal objects are comprehensible as a system of abstract relations and relata. Such an analysis discloses a realm of eternal objects as the "general fact of systematic mutual relatedness."[60] As pure potentials, eternal objects have an individual essence and a relational essence. As an individual, we discern the definite self-identity of an eternal object, and as relational, we understand its status as a relatum in the general scheme of relationships. In their relational essences, eternal objects are purely internal relations. Whitehead thus makes the point that: "Since the relationships of A to other eternal objects stand determinately in the essence of A, it follows that they are internal relations."[61] These relations stand as equally determinate and mutually dependent. For example, all the particular shades of color are internally related with respect to their common relational essence, color. But as internally related, these particular shades of color "do not involve the individual essences of the eternal objects; they involve *any* eternal objects as relata, subject to the proviso that these relata have the requisite relational essences."[62] In their relational essences, we can understand how eternal objects are related without reference to their individual essences.

The internal/external distinction is now applied to the relation between individual and relational essence such that generic objects are always externally related to more particular ones. Quality is external to color, color to blue, and blue to sky blue. But the particular eternal objects are internally related to the generic ones. Every shade of sky blue must be a shade of blue, a color, and a quality, and is therefore internally related to the higher generic objects. Every color, on the other hand, is not necessarily blue or sky blue. So color, as a general class of eternal objects, must be conceived as independent and external to the more specific eternal objects.[63]

Whitehead's whole point of introducing individual and relational essences was put forth to explain "how there can be internal relations, seeing that we admit finite truths."[64] One might suppose that he had in mind some general principle of absolute idealism where nothing short of an interrelated Whole will give us any truth at all. Since "everything must depend upon everything else" we must know everything to know anything. But granted Whitehead's solution, that the relationships between eternal objects as bare relata are comprehensible without reference to their respective individual essences, the claim is "palpably untrue."

If we look to Bradley as the chief expositor of such a doctrine, we find that the problem only vaguely resembles one of his central tenets, that the Absolute is the only true Subject of any judgment, and it is only by postulating this ultimate Subject that we can obtain any final truth. Finite, individual truths, for Bradley, are only appearances cut from the harmonious texture of the Absolute and must be understood as degrees of truth at best. But aside from this rough affinity, the problem does not address Bradley in any direct manner since he argued that *all* relations are contradictory—external and internal. In this respect, Bradley's response to Whitehead would be the same as that he gave Russell. However, insofar as Whitehead admits internal and external relations into his realm of eternal objects, we must explain how his view escapes Bradley's criticisms. We cannot appeal to a doctrine of "perishing" at this level as we did in the case of actual occasions. Eternal objects "stand determinately" as atemporal possibilities.

One fairly substantial discussion in the chapter on abstraction in *Science and the Modern World* seems to address the problem of Bradley's argument (2). As we recall, this argument involves the idea that any quality, in virtue of being related to others, must involve an infinite fission of grounds and consequents. The terms of internal relations consist of parts that are externally related, and so on *ad infinitum*.

Whitehead proposes the idea of an abstractive hierarchy where eternal objects are ordered in terms of grades of complexity. At the base of the hierarchy, there are eternal objects whose individual essences are simple. A particular shade of red, for example, is defined as simple because it is a definite shade that does not admit of further analysis of components. From the base, grades of complexity are ordered according to the complexity of components, and as we pass from the grade of simple eternal objects to higher and higher grades of complexity, we pass to higher grades of abstraction.

This appears to answer Bradley because the idea of a base of simplicity prevents an internal regress. A complex eternal object (turquoise, or the C major triad: C—E—G) may involve a multiplicity of other simpler eternal objects, but these are finally resolved into terminal instances at the base of the hierarchy where the grade of zero complexity is reached. Whitehead regards such a base of simple eternal objects as incapable of further analysis into components. In other words, it is incomprehensible that such eternal objects could have more fundamental constituents. A primary color red or a simple note C are the basic eternal objects from which more complex ones are constructed. From this base the hierarchy may be infinite or finite depending on the type of eternal objects investigated, but the base itself is not infinitely divisible.

The problem with this solution, from Bradley's point of view, is that the postulation of a base of simple essences does not prevent such eternal objects from fracturing into further parts once they are viewed as related. A simple eternal object is still a quality that must be conceived in its relation to other eternal objects, and as related, it must involve parts, namely, the fission of further qualities and relations that results from the initial relation.

In a certain sense Whitehead and Bradley are at cross-purposes here since Whitehead contends that the analysis of eternal objects is a pure abstraction. In this respect, the eternal objects are "devoid of real togetherness: they remain within their 'isolation' "[65] As bare relata that make up the skeletal structure, they are only objects of conceptual analysis and not instantiations in the concrete process. This means that Whitehead is not here concerned with the question of how qualities are related in a relational situation; he is constructing a system of logical classification and asking how eternal objects form various hierarchies. But even if we do view Bradley's argument as applying to Whitehead's project here, it is not at all clear why a quality as related must be fractured into parts. Bradley's point was that an internal relation must be contradictory because such a quality in this relation must have a difference on which distinction is based and involve a distinctness that results from connection. Although this distinction itself is at best obscure, some sense can be made of the notion that a quality retains its distinctness in a relation, while at the same time, it is defined by that relation.[66] But it does not follow that this necessarily involves parts within a quality.

Whitehead, in fact, seems to acknowledge something of this sort in his notion of relational and individual essences. An eternal object retains its definite identity in its individual essence, while at the same time, as a relatum in the general scheme of relationships, it necessarily involves a reference to other eternal objects in its relational essence. But these two aspects of qualities do not involve separate parts.

For Whitehead the realm of eternal objects and the interrelatedness of eternal objects within is based on his prior analysis of mathematics as an abstract science. Just as the internal structure of mathematics shows how quantities represented by the variables are not treated independently but rather are understood as a complex network of interrelations, in abstraction, eternal objects are internally related in an abstractive hierarchy. But while they remain related in such ways, they are also particular individuals that retain their identity in possibility and among diverse applications in actuality. We discern in conceptual analysis both individuality and relatedness.

In conclusion then, while Bradley argued that generally all individual terms and their relations must be seen as contradictory, Whitehead was concerned with a mathematical cosmology that would explain large-scale structures of abstraction and applications to concrete nature. For him this involved a complex structure in the universe where actuality and change require reference to possibility and permanence. This very point is, in fact, emphasized in his essay "Mathematics and the Good" when he says:

> The notion of the essential relatedness of all things is the primary step in understanding how finite entities require the unbounded universe, and how the universe acquires meaning and value by reason of its embodiment of the activity of finitude.[67]

Possibility (the unbounded universe) is mere vacancy apart from the intrinsic value added to the world by each actual occasion. Actuality and finitude add definiteness and value to what was merely unrealized potential.

Throughout this chapter, I have argued for the reality of various forms of relatedness constituting the essential structure of Whitehead's cosmology. My central focus has been Whitehead's notion of the concrete asymmetry of actual occasions, from which the more complex and increasingly abstract forms of relatedness were derived. Bradley's antirelational arguments were therefore rejected. Analysis does tell us something important about reality and the structure of 'feeling'; it gives order and direction to what James calls the "blooming, buzzing confusion." Moreover it enriches our interpretation once we return to immediacy. As Dorothy Emmet has put the point: "Relational thought could tell us nothing, nor even be of practical value, unless its symbolism had some kind of relevant reference to distinctions in the real."[68] Thought must be a symbolic representation of the forms and distinctions within reality itself; conceptual form and perceptual form must complement each other in the central task of understanding the universe. Of course, Whitehead was never dogmatic about perfecting such symbolic representations. Like Bradley, he is well aware of the limitations of finite knowledge and the distortion involved in the analytic slicing of experience. But, unlike Bradley, he held that the voyage of philosophy, and of thought, not only involves the discovery of the higher generalities, but also the discovery of the finer, subtler distinctions.

CHAPTER 5

Extension and Whole-Part Relations

EVENTS VERSUS SUBSTANCE

In *Process and Reality*, Whitehead argues that "the emotional appetitive elements in our conscious experience are those which most closely resemble the basic elements of all physical experience."[1] We shall assume that by "resemble" Whitehead here means some degree of sentient experience that characterizes the most rudimentary facts of physical existence. But can an ontology of "events," or throbs of experience, ranging from the most basic to a complexity of the sort that make up human consciousness, form the basis of the enduring objects of our perceptual experience? In other words, how can the basic ontology of actual occasions make up the hard material bodies of our everyday world and account for the system of nature?

Insofar as Bradley remained neutral on the question of panpsychism but most definitely held that the basis of all reality is sentient through and through, he is faced with the same problem. But the individual character of events we shall defend here is obviously at odds with Bradley's conception. Since, for him, nature is but one part of the wholeness of 'feeling', namely, the object side of the centre of experience, physical objects in extension are nothing but convenient abstractions.[2]

This chapter will present an expansion and defense of the section on panpsychism in chapter 2. The central focus is the superiority of the doctrine of event-pluralism over a materialist or substance ontology. Also, granted the main argument of our last chapter—that relations are necessary to articulating the connections of experience—we shall pursue a comprehensive theory of extension and whole-part relations via Whitehead's theory of society and cosmic epochs. This theory is important because it contrasts the way Whitehead conceives of the universe as an infinite plurality against Bradley's conception of the Absolute as the final container and end of relations. But before this is taken up, let us pursue the basic contrast between the theory of events and the theory of material substance.

P. F. Strawson has argued at length for an ontology of material substance in his influential book, *Individuals*. In fact, Strawson argues that the concept of material substance is basic, explicitly contrasting this conception to one in which events are basic. According to Strawson, objects, or material bodies, are primary, and events in which these bodies participate are merely adjectival. Following Aristotle, Strawson holds that the particulars that make up the framework of space-time—men, trees, houses, animals, plants, etc.—are bodies. These are the basic particulars, or individuals, because only they satisfy certain essential conditions of reference, namely, identification and reidentification.

Strawson insists that to talk meaningfully we must talk about worldly particulars, both individually and specifically. Our ability to talk about anything hinges on our being able to identify what we are talking about. By the use of demonstrative terms, we identify this or that individual as unique. As he argues:

> We can make it clear to each other what or which particular things our discourse is about because we can fit together each others reports and stories into a single picture of the world; and the framework of that picture is a unitary spatio-temporal framework, of one temporal and three spatial dimensions. Hence, as things are, particular-identification in general rests ultimately on the possibility of locating the particular things we speak of in a single unified spatio-temporal system.[3]

In short, identification by demonstrative terms rests on an agreement among a community of language users that share a unified spatio-temporal system. This constitutes a common conceptual framework of basic particulars. In order to secure a unitary scheme of this kind, basic objects of reference, namely, those on which all reference depends, must be capable of reidentification. That is, we must be able to refer on different occasions to individuals and recognize them as the same as those encountered on a previous occasion.[4]

Now, to claim that certain particulars are basic in an ontological scheme, we mean that all other particulars are ultimately reducible to them. Everything else that exists is in some sense a construction out of them. Hence, from Strawson's point of view, the material bodies that are accessible to observation, occupy a public space-time framework, and endure through time as the same individuals are the basic particulars from which everything else is derived. They are identified independently of particulars of other categories; but the particulars of these other categories cannot be identified without reference to them.[5] Strawson argues, therefore, that such things as theoretical constructs, processes, events, and subjective states of consciousness depend essentially on identifying references to the larger corporeal bodies of our perceptual experiences. For instance, talk about electrons and protons depends on identifying references to the electromagnetic effects of, say, magnets and chunks of uranium ore, while talk about private experiences and states of consciousness—pain, happiness, and boredom—depend on identifying references to the larger class of corporeal bodies, namely, persons.

Obviously Strawson's category preference and his criteria for locating basic particulars are in direct opposition to the ontology defended in the present work. Strawson's program, however, depends largely upon an acceptance of a restricted (or conservative) conception of metaphysics. He describes himself as engaged in "descriptive metaphysics," that is, as merely characterizing the conceptual scheme allegedly embodied in the language we use in everyday discourse. This of course rules out any attempt at detailed explanation of the origin and nature of the universe. The descriptive metaphysician is "content to describe the actual structure of our thought about the world." So from the start, his procedure is at odds with a revisionary scheme that takes events as basic. In describing the structure of our thought, Strawson assumes that common categories by which we understand the world are adequate for answering ontological questions. Moreover, he assumes that our conceptual scheme is constant over time and between different languages. In his view, it is commonplace of the least refined thinking and the indispensable core of the most sophisticated human beings.

Such a "revisionary" metaphysician as Whitehead, however, is setting out to question the adequacy of our common conceptual scheme, and, along with it, the ordinary language we use to identify individuals, at least, insofar as we see this as a procedure

for penetrating the nature of reality. Whitehead also rejects
any conceptual invariance of the sort that Strawson maintains.
He is more concerned with a new conceptual scheme that is more
adequate as a foundation for the sciences. His ontological priority works such that substances and properties are dependent on
events.

Let us then proceed to evaluate Strawson's thesis in light of
Whitehead's view. First, we should examine the contention that
material bodies are the basic particulars from the point of view of
identification. It will be simpler here to confine our responses to a
Whiteheadian point of view, though on many points, Bradley
would be in close accord. We should also recall that the term
event in Whitehead's system stands for a nexus of actual occasions forming the historic route in the life of some physical object. As he says: "An actual occasion is the limiting type of event
with only one member."[6] For our purposes, however, we shall use
the generic term *event* as interchangeable with *actual occasion*.

By his emphasis on identity-by-reference, Strawson falls into
the trap of taking what is clear and distinct to presentational
immediacy as fundamental. This is one of the striking facts about
his approach to category preference; that is, his defence of the
grosser physical bodies immediately present to perception. But
are these the true individuals? For Strawson, the point hinges on
the ability of a community of language users to get across to one
another what their discourse is about. They must be able to
identify and reidentify the basic objects of reference. But of course
the central question here is: Why should linguistic agreement
serve as the ultimate criterion for identifying the basic particulars
of reality? No doubt ordinary language is less accurate for describing event-processes, or flows of experience. But it does not
follow from this that events cannot constitute the basis of reality.
It only says something about the development of language in
serving our most practical needs.

From the point of view of the event ontology, identity-by-
reference is not the real issue. Physical bodies identified and
reidentified over a given period of time need not be self-identical
in any absolute sense. We refer to these bodies as more or less the
same—"Professor Smart has lost more hair"; "My brother has
grown two inches"; "That cup has lost much of its original color."

We have no trouble recognizing change in enduring bodies, but it is only for the most practical purposes that we refer to these bodies as "the same." In fact, if it were not for certain recurrent features of process (i.e., the eternal objects in Whitehead's system—colors, sounds, shapes, etc.), we would not be able to reidentify physical bodies at all. In the continuous flux of events, it is a dominance of inherited characteristics that is recognized by a speaker who reidentifies a body as the same one identified before. But the sense-objects recognized here are not the basic particulars. Objects are ingredients, the *whats* of events. They provide structures for event-sequences, but they are not the basis of their own survival.

Strawson might counter this move by insisting that the subjects of the above sentences have already introduced concrete particulars ("Professor Smart," "my brother," "that cup"). The predicates merely qualify changes or processes that have occurred to self-identical individuals. In the case of the cup, the subject of the sentence introduces a particular whereas the predicate, "has lost much of its original color," does not of itself presuppose any fact.[7] But on this point it must be noted that the adequacy of the subject-predicate distinction and the metaphysics it presupposes is precisely what is at issue. In this case, the substance-attribute distinction is not vindicated by an analysis of grammar; it is simply shown to be embedded in the very structure of our language.

Two points must be made in this connection, and both center upon different aspects of Whitehead's general claim that ordinary language actually distorts immediate experience and hinders our ability to get at the basis of reality. First, the technique of identifying subjects and predicates tends to reinforce our habit of viewing the world in terms of static individuals qualified by various properties. The tendency of natural language is, first, to isolate a substantial material entity and then to describe it by its accidental changes. But the basic duality inherent in the subject-predicate form of statement cannot grasp the very dynamics of process. And it is only a historical accident that the conception of substance has reigned supreme in the Western tradition, first as a consequence of the subject-predicate structure of Greek, and then of the dominance of Aristotelian logic.

Second, and closely related to the first point, the isolation of individuals by ordinary language suggests the complete abstraction from any environment. Such abstraction, however, neglects the whole background against which individuals are selected. It is on this point that Whitehead's philosophy of language accords with the most basic concept behind Bradley's logic. The delusive completeness of simple facts in demonstrative propositions (Bradley's analytic judgment of sense) does not express anything ultimate from the point of view of general metaphysics. Simple facts or individuals in propositions require the entirety of relations in the systematic environment in order to determine a truth value, and this is quite impossible. As Whitehead puts the point: "every proposition proposing a fact must, in its complete analysis, propose the general character of the universe required for that fact."[8]

Whitehead would not wish to deny that the grosser enduring objects and their properties are the primary objects of discourse; but this, in itself, is no ultimate criterion for determining basic particulars. Whitehead therefore rejects Strawson's connection of ontological priority with identifiability. Clearly we are dealing with two very different issues, one concerning the usefulness of ordinary language, and the other concerning basic particulars from which the rest of the ontology is constructed. As we have argued, the essence of reality will always elude the grasp of a language designed to describe static objects in various spatial relations. It was on this point that Whitehead, at the expense of great obscurity, produced a "revisionary metaphysics" by creating a language to fit his novel vision of an event universe. Contrary to Strawson, there is little point in examining the actual use of words if our aim is to uncover the basis of reality. Language is a tool required by philosophy, but it is always subject to revision. In this respect, the metaphysician cannot share the ordinary man's faith in the adequacy of everyday language in describing reality. We fashion our language and concepts to fit reality, not the other way around. Strawson thus seems to have it backwards when he argues that the revisionary metaphysician is at the service of the descriptive metaphysician; for the latter is confined to the dictionary, while the former expands the existing repertoire by adjusting the language to express new meanings.

Strawson's argument against an ontology of events rests on the claim that such states or conditions are always parasitic on particulars of other types, namely, material bodies. Births and deaths happen to particular creatures. Bangs, flashes, and battles are all products, so to speak, of material bodies in motion. So from the point of view of identification, material objects provide the basis for talk about events. Furthermore, reidentification of events demands reidentification of material objects, but not vice-versa. For Strawson, events are conceptually dependent on material objects and can be done away with in a way the objects cannot because events cannot provide "a single, comprehensive and continuously usable framework of reference" of the kind provided by physical objects. It is clear, however, that Strawson's examples are not the sorts of events that would make an event ontology plausible. And even if we confine our investigation to the larger macroscopic events of perceptual experience, (usually identified in ordinary speech by verbs and adverbial clauses), we do find them to be the objects of reference in ordinary language.

While sharing Strawson's belief in our common conceptual scheme, Donald Davidson has taken issue with him on ontological priority of objects. Davidson finds that various grammatical structures and their logical forms designate event structures by identity and individuation. Events can be quantified over in definite descriptions and therefore exist as particulars.[9] Hence Davidson argues that there is no reason to assign second-rank status to events; while there is a conceptual dependence of the category of events on the category of objects, there is also a symmetrical dependence of the category of objects on the category of events.[10] But granted this admission, neither Strawson nor Davidson have considered how material bodies themselves might be composed of aggregates of events mainly because their concept of the event is too narrowly conceived or, in some cases, misconceived.

Strawson's chapter on "Sounds" is a good example of how his case against an event ontology is misconceived. Here he attempts to construct an ontology in which material bodies are not the basic particulars, and concludes that a purely auditory world would make discourse impossible because we would not be able to distinguish between ourselves as subjects of experience and other items in the world distinct from ourselves. But the conceptual problem posed by the possibility of a "No-Space World" in which all the sensory items are auditory is misconstrued as an argument against an event ontology. Events that make up the physical world cannot be deprived of their extensive relations in space, so sounds are rather poor examples of the types of events that might plausibly function as basic particulars. In short, the kinds of events Strawson discusses throughout his book are either phenomenal or the larger macroscopic variety.[11] Davidson, on the other hand, is only interested in a certain variety of events that squares with his adverbial theory and that ultimately provides a basis for his theory of action.

Hartshorne has argued that the very logic that drives us from genus to species to individual is the same logic that should drive us one step further to the event.[12] Just as the individual is more determinate than the species, so is the event more determinate than the individual. Strawson seems to have accepted a rather arbitrary definition of *individual* that serves our linguistic purposes, but even biologists recognize that our system of classification is a artificial structure of pigeonholes serving the pragmatic purpose of recording observations in a convenient manner.[13] In many respects the clusters we label "genus" and "species" are not always clear cut. And, even if we confine ourselves to individuals, there are grey areas that are very problematic. At what point in the life of a tadpole does it become a frog, the caterpillar a butterfly? Similarly, when does the embryo become a fetus, the fetus a person? When does a human being cease to be a person? Religious and state institutions, in their attempt to define an individual, have not found adequate answers to these last two questions. Why should we accept uncritically the conventions of ordinary language? The evidence seems to point to a more determinate basic particular than the individual.

If we accept the notion that unit-events form the basis of the temporal process, we find that individuals can be defined in terms of a certain dominance of character or recognizable sameness of pattern passed within the event-sequences. In Whitehead's view, for example, what we recognize are eternal objects. They are identified and reidentified in definite space-time regions, but the events that contain them are unrepeatable. The self-identity of a physical object or person across time that Strawson seeks to vindicate is simply an unwarranted survival of the concept of substance from Aristotle and the scholastic tradition. It is a presupposition required for social intercourse, but metaphysically it is unfounded. If we require a basis for moral responsibility or ownership in legal theory, all that is needed is that a person or physical object remain more or less the same by the fact that the unique line of inheritance is traceable. An earlier event is internally related to a present one, but there is nothing that is wholly the same individual.

COSMOLOGICAL OUTLOOK

The event ontology is no doubt an alternative to established orthodoxy. But it is quite persuasive as a foundation for physical objects and the space-time framework. In the 1920s Whitehead, Russell, and Broad all became champions of this view because they were convinced that the theory was more compatible with the emerging relativity theory. Instead of conceiving material bodies as the basic particulars within the framework of spatial and temporal relations, an ontology of events means that physical objects are constructs of event-particulars in a space and time of their own making. This ontology takes seriously the meaning of the twentieth-century concept of space-time, for the becoming of each event carries with it a definite quantum of extended space-time, and each discloses a causal background from which it came.

Working from the unit-event as our basic particular, we can construct various levels of physical objects—from the microscopic, subatomic level all the way up to star systems and cosmic epochs—by the manner in which events are united by their more special or general characteristics. This was a central aim in Whitehead's cosmological theory in which he attempted a unification of the special sciences in terms of one coherent and systematic account of social organization.

His own attempt to build up physical objects from the basis of events seems to have been highly influenced by the promising developments in physics at the turn of this century. While William James supplied the psychological basis for the connectedness of experience, the concept of the flux of energy in an electromagnetic field seemed to provide the necessary physical analogue for the doctrine of prehension. We shall discuss two important aspects of the physical theory here, namely, the implications for the concept of space-time and the dematerialization of nature.

When J. C. Maxwell formulated the equations governing the propagation of waves of radiation in the electromagnetic field, the unexpected result for the scientific community was the elimination of bits of matter as the self-identical supports for physical properties. This was the beginning of the breakdown of the old dichotomy of atoms and the void; for the concept of a field of force means that space is made up of various stresses and tensions that transmit energy. The notion of empty space as the mere vehicle of spatial interconnections is therefore abandoned as a fundamental principle in physical explanations. The field is rather a medium by which electric or magnetic objects can have an effect over a distance. It is something that pervades space and contains recognizable routes of energy. These routes are sometimes called "energy vectors" because, at each point, the passing of energy in the flux has a quantitative flow and definite direction.[14]

As Whitehead points out, the concept of continuity was dominant in Maxwell's theory. It seemed as if the concept of a field had done away with the atomistic conception of nature dominant in classical physics, but when J. J. Thompson and Ernest Rutherford detected protons, electrons, and photons as unit charges of electricity, the atomistic conception emerged again as an indispensable part of science. These subatomic particles were introduced to account for the many different chemical elements formed by various combinations of the basic types of subatomic particles. For example, the number of electrons revolving round the nucleus in an atom defined the numerical place occupied by the given element in the Periodic Table.

With the introduction of quantum theory at the beginning of this century, the atomistic conception seemed to be challenged again by a certain insubstantial and unthinglike behavior of elementary particles. This theory was developed to account for phenomena previously unexplained. (e.g. Why does emission of radiation occur at some definite intensities and not at others? Why do different elements emit radiation at distinct wavelengths?)

According to quantum theory, such phenomena are explained by the notion that energy of all types occurs in quanta or minimal packets. Atoms are then to be understood in terms of waves of radiation that they can emit or absorb, and this occurs at nonuniform spans of time. The reason why a simple particle theory of the atom, using ordinary mechanics and electromagnetic theory, does not succeed is that the electron cannot be considered simply as a particle. That is, since it cannot have both a well-defined position and velocity, it must be seen in part as a wave.[15] The orbits of electrons are to be regarded as series of detached positions rather than continuous lines. This is what is meant by quantum "leaps" or "jumps."

From classical mechanics, the idea that particles have a definite size, shape, and position was therefore abandoned. The emphasis now turns on pulses of energy that have an approximate location of space-time, and interact in fields that bear and transmit the forces of nature. This idea seemed to correspond with the earlier idea of vectors describing routes of transmission, but the routes are now discontinuous. The notion that light and other electromagnetic radiations are transmitted as continuous trains of waves is replaced by the idea that radiation can only be emitted in pulses.

With respect to Whitehead's understanding of quantum physics, much of his thought took shape before the detailed elaboration of the theory had been achieved. His interpretation derives from the earlier atomic models and theories of Planck and Bohr, not the new quantum theory of 1925–1927 proposed by Heisenberg and Schrödinger.[16] But it is quite clear that he had attempted to integrate much of the field and quantum theories into the structure of his general cosmological outlook.

First, in Whitehead's theory, we recall that the extensive continuum provides the general framework of real potentiality rendered specific or actual with the becoming of each event. This means that the whole system of space-time literally grows out of the way that events are systematically related to one another in nature. Since each event carries its own quantum of space and time, the void is clearly impossible. It is, in fact, explicitly ruled out by the "ontological principle" which requires everything to be somewhere in actuality.[17] Even so-called empty space is filled with activity; it is just that such events involve no specialized characteristics resulting from the negligible amount of eternal objects.[18] The universe is therefore one endless field of interaction, though, in Whitehead's view, the electromagnetic features of energy are only characteristic of our limited cosmic epoch.

Second, the emphasis on pulses of energy in physical theory suggested that matter had been identified with energy, and energy with sheer activity.[19] With the displacement of matter from its primary position, nature is therefore to be understood in terms of dynamic processes standing in various complex relations. Whitehead remarks that: "In place of the Aristotelian notion of the procession of forms, [this new concept] has substituted the notion of the forms of process."[20]

The metaphysical analogue to the physical concept of an energy vector is Whitehead's concept of prehension where routes of influence or emotional energy are passed from event to event. In his metaphysics, events or actual occasions account for the atomistic aspect of nature, while the extensive features of the space-time continuum account for continuity. Like quantum theory, Whitehead holds that all physical experience happens in leaps or definite epochs of becoming. But what is particularly revealing about the findings of quantum mechanics is that, at the base of things, the discontinuous existence of fundamental particles forms the continuous existence of the larger physical bodies. Undoubtedly, Whitehead found this idea crucial in explaining how his basic ontology of events could form the various levels of enduring 'societies.' He says, in fact, that his cosmological theory is "perfectly consistent with the demands for discontinuity which have been urged from the side of physics."[21] Physical reality is, at most, quasi-continuous, as successive leaps or vibrations of energy fuse together to form physical objects perceived by us as continuous.

This first level of rudimentary physical activity, that of subatomic particles, is not to be identified with the basic events or actual occasions of Whitehead's metaphysics. What is observable to the physicist, the effects of subatomic particles in the electromagnetic field, is, on Whitehead's view, multiple interactions of events with an electromagnetic character. And, as he argues:

> The notion of physical energy, which is at the base of physics, must then be conceived as an abstraction from the complex energy, emotional and purposeful, inherent in the subjective

form of the final synthesis in which each occasion completes itself.[22]

Scientific inquiry obviously involves very high degrees of abstractions that remove us from the concrete real things of nature. From this it should be clear that Whitehead would not appeal to physics to seek the final word on the metaphysical primacy of events. That is, since physics deals in high abstractions, the substance/event issue cannot be settled here. But Whitehead does hold that physics has come to conclusions that are in much more accordance with a metaphysics that gives the concept of an event a primary place.

In my discussion of Whitehead's conformity to various findings of twentieth-century physics, I have avoided the issue of the sentient character of events in order to concentrate on the more general cosmological implications. As we have argued earlier, this issue belongs to the special province of metaphysical inquiry.[23] Admittedly, the hardest gap for the panpsychist to fill is that between the occasions of experience immediately present to consciousness, and the first level of physical activity. On the one hand, there is the emotional energy entertained in life, and on the other, the physical flux of energy in nature. But, as Whitehead continually argued throughout his later metaphysical works: "neither physical nature nor life can be understood unless we fuse them together as essential factors in the composition of 'really real' things whose interconnections and individual characters constitute the universe."[24]

TRANSMUTATION AND THE THEORY OF SOCIETY

At no point in the writings of Bradley do we encounter an explanation of various levels of wholes and parts in the organization of physical reality. Since for the most part, Bradley remains open as to whether the whole of nature is composed of various degrees of finite centres of experience (i.e., those of a nonhuman sort), no such explanation is required in his metaphysical system. If it were so, perhaps Bradley would have offered some type of theory bordering on cosmology, but it remains doubtful since, for him, this would be an attempt to explain the character of finite appearances. At most we are to understand that finite centres and their consciousness of themselves as parts finally lose their independent natures once "transmuted and suppressed" in one all-absorbing experience of the Absolute. The detailed apprehension of this fusion is, however, quite beyond our capabilities.[25] As Bradley himself says:

> There really is within the Absolute a diversity of finite centres. There really is within finite centres a world of objects. . . . These things are realities, and yet, because imperfect, they are but appearances which differ in degree. That they are supplemented and without loss are all made good absolutely in the Whole, we are led to conclude. But how in detail this is accomplished, and exactly what the diversity of finite centres means in the end, is beyond our knowledge.[26]

So, for Bradley, we might say that the *how* is always unnecessary once the general principle is forced upon us. [27] And this not only means how the final unity is accomplished by the Absolute, but also how the whole of nature is arranged by finite centres, human or nonhuman.

Though, in the end, the notion of transmutation of finite actualities into one all-absorbing experience will be a crucial doctrine for our final comparison between Bradley and Whitehead (chapter 7), it is fairly clear that Bradley's agnosticism regarding the variety and linkage of the centres is given a reasonable basis in Whitehead's system. Much of this depends on the general position taken on relations, and if relations are indeed real, various levels of social organization in nature can be constructed by the general relations of extensive connection.

Other absolute idealists, particularly those inclined toward a panpsychist interpretation of the world, have attempted to give some explanation as to how various levels of sentience form wholes that may or may not themselves be sentient organisms. Royce, for example, held that everything "enjoys" a certain sentience, but depending on the arrangement in the scale of organic and inorganic forms, the specious present experienced varies in different stretches. In his view, the life of experience pulsates throughout the arteries of Being.[28] Given such interpretations where genuine individuality within the Whole is emphasized, we find some attempt to explain how the "arteries" are arranged. At least here some line of thought is open to the monist who has not been restrained by denying the reality of relations. Royce, for example, accepted a view of relations that was compatible with the Absolute and therefore disagreed with Bradley about how much detailed structure was possible.

Whitehead, on the other hand, provided a very detailed account of organization in nature that was based on observations from physics, chemistry, biology, and astronomy. Actual occasions form 'societies' by their common characteristics, and these are arranged into various levels of organisms and environments, or systems within systems. We have already mentioned how Whitehead conceives of the first level of physical activity as multiple interactions of electromagnetic occasions forming routes of energy. But this is still the microscopic world as far as human perception is concerned. What we require is an explanation of how the occasions form various layers of organisms of organisms (electrons, atoms, molecules, cells, . . .), until we arrive at the enduring bodies of ordinary perception (stones, plants, animals, planets, . . .), and finally, galaxy clusters, cosmic epochs, and pure extension.

But before we proceed any further, one point should certainly be clear. That is, 'societies' are the things that endure, but they must not be confused with the completely real things which are the actual occasions.[29] This distinguishes his view from that of Strawson and others following Aristotle's conception of substance.

What then needs to be explained is why we perceive tables, chairs, and trees and not multitudes of actual occasions in the immediate environment. (Analogously, this point applies equally to the purely physical interpretation of the world in terms of electrons or routes of energy.) Whitehead makes the transition from the microscopic world of actual occasions to the macroscopic world of our perceptual experience by his notion of transmutation, whereby occasions in any one physical body are prehended as a unity.[30] When we perceive any macroscopic entity, he argues that we prehend an aggregate of many occasions as one final unity. An individual is discerned in the mass of actual occasions present to consciousness by the way the perceiver integrates the many members of the 'society' and produces one transmuted 'feeling'. This is possible because the members of the 'society' share a certain dominance of characteristics, the identity of pattern of the ingredient eternal objects. Hence, we are able to pick out the chair, as opposed to the empty space around it, because of the dominance of certain eternal objects shared by the members of the chair that are prehended by us as a unity.

This idea of the many-functioning-as-one is not, perhaps, altogether different from the way the eye fuses a multiplicity of dots which make up a picture. For example, when one views a painting by the French Impressionist, Georges Seurat, dots of color blend together to form more complex colors, and at just the right distance from the canvas, the admiring onlooker perceives figures and shapes instead of the individual dots. The final result is one transmuted 'feeling'—the emotion of that particular painting resulting from the synthesis of colors and shapes.

So for many purposes, a nexus of actualities can be treated as though it were one actuality. This is what happens at several levels of the extensive continuum where some particular entity or group is isolated for the investigation at hand—molecules, cells, a piece of rock, the human body, or the planet Mars. But what is quite clear to Whitehead is that, in this process of abstraction, we should not neglect the importance of the interrelations within nature that make this possible.

Our sense perceptions, Whitehead argues, are often vague and confused.[31] They omit any discrimination of the fundamental activities within nature, even though, via symbolic reference, they do pick out the broad outlines of social order. Whatever properties we are able to give to any particular body, they approximate, more or less, the type of order that dominates among the members which impose common characteristics on one another.

Whitehead specifically defines a 'society' as a nexus of social order in which:

> (i) there is a common element of form illustrated in the definiteness of each of its included actual entities, and (ii) this common element of form arises in each member of the nexus by reason of the conditions imposed upon it by its prehensions of some other members of the nexus, and (iii) these prehensions impose that condition of reproduction by reason of their inclusion of positive feelings of that common form.[32]

These three conditions provide the main point of a 'society', namely, that it is self-sustaining. The 'society' reproduces itself by the fact that the members of the 'society' must positively prehend those eternal objects that not only define the 'society' in question but ensure its continued survival. In this respect it is quite clear that a 'society' is not simply an aggregate of mutually contemporary occasions, but rather multiple lines of inheritance. Not only must there be a certain quantity of contemporaries at any one time, certain genetic conditions of prehension must also be satisfied for the 'society' to endure through time.[33]

'Societies' can be simple or vastly complex. The simplest ones are those with "personal order," in which the members are ordered serially. The most specialized cases of these 'societies' are the routes of electronic or protonic actualities in which the choices are extremely limited. Here, there is only a single line of inheritance. But these simple 'societies' form the base of higher 'societies', namely electrons and protons, and thus begins the hierarchy of societies "of increasing width of prevalence, the more special societies being included in the wider societies."[34]

Whitehead therefore introduces the idea of a structured 'society' as one which includes subordinate 'societies' and/or nexūs. He says that:

> A structured society consists in the patterned intertwining of various nexūs with markedly diverse defining characteristics. Some of these nexūs are of lower types than others, and some will be of markedly higher types. There will be 'subservient' nexūs and the 'regnant' nexūs within the same structured society. This structured society will provide the immediate environment which sustains each of its sub-societies, subservient and regnant alike.[35]

A cell, for example, is structured in the sense that it is a 'society' that harbors the existence of lower, more specialized 'societies'—at one level molecules, at another atoms, and so on. So the higher 'society', (the cell) is regnant, and functions as an environment for the lower level, (the molecules), while the lower 'societies' are subservient and function as organisms for the higher level. This reciprocity of whole and parts applies throughout the various levels of order in the extensive continuum—working outward in terms of environments or inward in terms of organisms. In this way, all 'societies' are enmeshed in a system of ever-widening characteristics and influence. The wider environment always provides the necessary conditions for the survival of the more special organism.

"A 'structured society' may be more or less 'complex' in respect to the multiplicity of its associated sub-societies and sub-nexūs and to the intricacy of their structural pattern."[36] It may be inorganic (crystals, rocks, planets, suns) or organic (cells, tomatoes, human beings). There is no absolute gap between these two categories; the distinction merely serves certain purposes where life may be important or unimportant.[37] For instance, in the first category of material bodies life is unimportant for the science of dynamics. But up and down the continuum we find that many apparently inorganic 'societies' sustain the organic ones, and organic 'societies' include subordinate inorganic ones. For example, the solar system sustains the planet earth, and living animals and plants sustain their arrangements of molecules and atoms.

If the 'society' in question forms one body and the subordinate 'societies' constitutive of it are all strands of enduring objects, it is said to be "corpuscular." A volume of gas may be a rather loose society in that it includes subordinate 'societies' (molecules, atoms), but the volume itself is not corpuscular even though the individual molecules are. Corpuscular 'societies', such as stones and billiard balls, consist of very low-level occasions that display no originality and thereby provide ideal instances of efficient causality for mechanics. As Whitehead says, they elicit "a massive average objectification of a nexus, while eliminating the detailed diversities of the various members of the nexus in question."[38] Thus the Castle Rock at Edinburgh changes very little as the same eternal objects are inherited from year to year, century to century. In this sense, it remains the same rock as seen by the Romans two thousand years ago, by Hume two hundred years ago, and by contemporary Edinburghers today. But sure enough, from the point of view of geological time, it is wearing away in proportion to the changes imposed upon it by the larger 'society', namely the planet earth.

Most 'societies' we come into contact with are democracies in the sense that their subordinate 'societies' function together without some central, unified mentality. Certain cell colonies, plants, ecosystems and most lower forms of many-celled animals are democracies. These organisms react to stimuli, but there is no central direction or unified control. Higher animals, however, are those with a dominant living nexus of personal order. In the case of the vertebrate animals, the nexus of occasions with a dominance of the mental pole arises out of the complex nervous system—here defined as a system of neural occasions eventually forming the neurons. And the intensity of this experience, we must presume, varies from species to species.

Whitehead's own account of psychological physiology (physiological psychology reversed) is indeed complex, and far exceeds the central theme of this section. Here we should only mention that the human being is an organic structured 'society' in which the dominant nexus is a purely temporal, single-line inheritance of actual occasions known as the "stream of consciousness"—or what Whitehead calls the "final percipient occasions" of human experience.[39] This results from a certain intensity of the subjective form in the nexus. As Peirce once said, it is a kind of "public spirit among the nerve cells." Throughout the course of this study, it has been our example of the flow of reality, but one which, unlike the more fundamental types, captures the vivid immediacy of the present awareness of itself.

Obviously Whitehead's views are a polar opposite to the materialist interpretations popular today, many of which have found stimulus from computer models of the brain and studies of the nervous system. But Whitehead's conception provides an equally plausible account of the mental-physical duality, and in many respects exceeds the one-sided accounts of physio-chemical functions of the brain.[40] From his point of view, the materialist merely operates within a limited region of structured 'societies', i.e., internal organs of the body and sub-'societies' such as molecules and nerve cells. But it is never quite clear how consciousness could evolve from the inert and essentially lifeless base of matter. As Whitehead argues, there is nothing to evolve because one set of external relations will be as good as any other set.[41]

To proceed with the more general considerations of this section, what makes Whitehead's philosophy an organic view of nature is this central idea of nested hierarchies of 'societies'; of smaller units of organisms nested in the larger ones, and the interdependence of wholes and parts. But in accordance with the one-way dependence of the temporal process, certain exchanges take place between the organisms and their environments in order that higher, more complex organisms can evolve from lower, more simple ones. That is, the wholes and parts function together such that the parts are modified in accordance with the plan of the whole, and the whole is modified by its internal constituents. Whitehead, on this matter, locates two sides of the mechanism involved in the development of nature. He says that (i) a given environment dominates its subordinate 'societies' such that the organisms adapt themselves to it, and (ii) the organisms create their own environment by a certain cooperation among themselves in producing the desired effect.[42] On the first point (i), an individual organism (of whatever level) is liable to have aspects of the larger pattern dominating its own being and thus experiences modifications of the larger pattern reflected in itself. Obviously such reactions to changing circumstances in the wider environment are of utmost importance for natural selection where adaption becomes crucial. But also (ii), organisms can change and mold the environment that defines them. To take a simple case, body cells, for example, alter their extracellular environment by exchanging chemicals, generating heat, and so on. The environment must therefore have a certain plasticity such that over a longer period of time a higher organism can evolve from changes that take place in the subordinate organisms. Changes at the lower level produce an increase of complexity, thus allowing the evolution of novel and more sophisticated organisms.[43]

So, in the end, the survival and evolution of organisms is dependent upon favorable conditions in the larger environment that allow the proliferation of its members (i.e., the development of a larger number of similar organisms that are productive to the environment itself), while extinction implies the lack of such conditions. That is, an organism dies out when the environment ceases to favor its existence. The deterioration of the environment is the deterioration of the very order that allows for its proliferation.

COSMIC EPOCHS AND THE ABSOLUTE

If we pursue the general principle of whole-part relations, organisms and environments, to the highest conceivable level, we could very well arrive at *one* final 'society' of the widest possible extension. Although Bradley does not arrive at his notion of the Absolute in quite this way, his general conclusion that there cannot be individuals or relations without some larger whole in which they are contained approaches this line of thought. Indeed it is not too far off the mark to think of Bradley's suprarelational Absolute as one cosmic Organism that functions as the largest environment for everything in existence.

But, for Bradley, this ultimate society is not in process or capable of evolution or decay. For him the final Reality is a timeless eternity in which all subordinate aspects are but finite appearances of the perfect order. From this perspective, the Absolute experiences the whole of existence in one frozen specious present. It contains process, but process is not reality. As Bradley puts the point in one of his more colorful passages:

> This one Reality . . . enters into, but is itself incapable of evolution and progress . . . progress and decay are alike incompatible with perfection . . . There is of course progress in the world, and there is also retrogression, but we cannot think that the Whole either moves on or backwards. The Absolute has no history of its own, though it contains histories without number . . . For nothing perfect, nothing genuinely real, can move. The Absolute has no seasons, but all at once bears its leaves, fruit and blossoms. Like our globe it always, and it never, has summer and winter.[44]

All subordinate aspects of existence essentially contribute the richness of diversity to that life of the one Reality, but there is no sense in which the internal appearances move the Absolute to some state or condition of novelty. The final order simply is what it is; there is no better or worse, for in Bradley's view, these adjectives are but constructions based on some given piece of finitude.

Within the Absolute, Bradley says, there is no logical objection to the possibility of an indefinite number of systems of space and time that have their own order but do not move on one another.[45] From the point of view of the type of spatio-temporal order we experience in our world, the order in these other logically possible worlds is very different but not totally inconceivable. They are experienced by the Absolute as transmuted into one harmonious unity but on their own each has an independent existence and does not causally interact with the others.

In many respects, though not wholly the same, this idea of alternative systems of spatio-temporal order comes into close accord with what Whitehead called "cosmic epochs." Our own epoch of space-time order he says is "that widest society of actual entities whose immediate relevance to ourselves is traceable."[46] But this is only one system of order that we can comprehend more or less by formulating the laws of nature. Like Bradley, Whitehead holds that there is no logical objection, or, indeed, a metaphysical objection, to an indefinite number of such systems. But for Whitehead, they are not all contemporaries in some larger system. We must conjecture that there were an infinite number of cosmic epochs that preceded our present one, and with the decay of the present order reigning in this cosmic society, there will be an infinite number of successors. There was no first event, nor will there be a final event.

Although we shall discuss, in some detail, Bradley's conception of these alternative systems in the first section of chapter 6, we shall here concentrate our attention on the much broader metaphysical picture.

One of the crucial points of disagreement between Whitehead and Bradley concerns the issue of whether Reality contains process, or whether process *is* reality. Given Bradley's remarks above, his answer is quite clear. All conflict, movement, evolution, and process are finally resolved in one all-embracing, and self-contained Whole. Whitehead's position, however, is indeed complex and sometimes perplexing aside from the obvious answer. In what follows we shall attempt to indicate some of the problems associated with his position and provide some clarification as to how they may be resolved.

Whereas in Bradley's monism, all relatedness is finally transmuted in one all-embracing cosmic Whole, in Whitehead's view, the layering of social order is potentially infinite. Beginning with our own cosmic epoch, he says, we discern a vast 'society' of electronic and protonic actualities set in a wider social context of four-dimensionality. Beyond this level there is a geometrical 'society' in which the axioms of geometry are discoverable. But his geometrical 'society' presupposes even wider 'societies' that fade from realization as they become more distanced from our innermost cosmic 'society', and our powers of intellectual discernment. At one level, Whitehead thinks, there is a 'society' of mere dimensionality, and then finally we arrive at the widest 'society' of order conceivable, namely, pure extension.[47]

As Whitehead explains this system of whole-part relations in the extensive continuum, he writes:

> In these general properties of extensive connection [whole-part relations and various types of geometrical elements], we discern the defining characteristic of a vast nexus extending far beyond our immediate cosmic epoch. It contains in itself other epochs, with more particular characteristics incompatible with each other. Then from the standpoint of our present epoch, the fundamental society in so far as it transcends our own epoch seems a vast confusion mitigated by the few, faint elements of order contained in its own defining characteristics of 'extensive connection.' We cannot discriminate its other epochs of vigorous order, and we merely conceive it as harboring the faint flush of the dawn of order in our own epoch. This ultimate, vast society constitutes the whole environment within which our epoch is set, so far as systematic characteristics are discernible by us in our present stage of development.[48]

Although it would be tempting to identify this one ultimate 'society' of pure extension with Bradley's Absolute, this is clearly not the case. For Whitehead explicitly says "there is no society in isolation."[49] And as he says regarding the boundless character of the extensive continuum, "There are always entities beyond entities because non-entity is no boundary."[50] Hence, the 'society' of pure extension is not to be thought of as a "final container," but rather as the largest *conceivable* 'society'. Perhaps "in the future the growth of theory may endow our successors with keener powers of discernment," but at this point in history, Whitehead views the 'society' of pure extension as the largest known whole.[51]

What then is beyond the 'societies' that constitute the physical and geometrical order of nature is unknown, or simply disorderly by our understanding of order, even though some sense of whole and part is still vaguely discerned. As Whitehead makes this point: "Beyond these societies there is disorder, where 'disorder' is a relative term expressing the lack of importance possessed by the defining characteristics of the societies in question beyond their own bounds."[52] Chaotic disorder simply means the lack of dominant definition in 'societies' beyond our comprehension.

But here a problem arises with regard to the increasing width of social order beyond our own epoch. That is, once we have transcended the level of the cosmic epoch, is there any sense in which these ultimate 'societies' can be understood to be in process? Does the geometrical 'society' change, such that the axioms that are self-evident to one cosmic epoch become totally different ones to another cosmic epoch? Or even more generally, is there any evolution or process in the 'society' of pure extension? Keeping in mind that the cosmological theory is only applicable to our particular cosmic epoch, the question then arises as to the metaphysical ultimacy of process in Whitehead's philosophy.

Considering the vastness of the universe, Whitehead does not ascribe to the extensive continuum anything more than the very general properties of extensiveness, divisibility, and the relation of whole and part. As he attempts to locate the ultimate metaphysical necessities in this scheme, he writes:

> Some general character of coordinate divisibility is probably an ultimate metaphysical character, persistent in every cosmic epoch of physical occasions. Thus some of the simpler characteristics of extensive connection, as here stated, are probably such ultimate metaphysical necessities. . . .
>
> The more ultimate side of this scheme, perhaps that side which is metaphysically necessary, is at once evident by the consideration of the mutual implication of extensive whole and extensive part. . . .
>
> In this general description of the states of extension, nothing has been said about physical time or physical space, or of the more general notion of creative advance. These are notions which presuppose the more general relationship of extension.[53]

With considerations of this sort we might be led to find an affinity with Bradley, for if only such general principles of extensive connection are metaphysically ultimate, then it seems that process and the creative advance apply to the very limited regions of the universe. But this would be contrary to the most fundamental notion in Whitehead's philosophy—that process *is* reality.

The difficulty can, I think, be cleared up with the crucial point that the scheme of extensive connection is an abstraction from the process. The layering of social order is derived from the base of actual occasions. As we recall from an earlier chapter, the extensive continuum is an abstract system of logical relations.[54] It is the first determination of order, of real potentiality. As we ascend the continuum to various levels of social order, extending outward spatially, we become more removed from the concrete actual occasions that atomize the continuum, to increasingly abstract levels, where the defining characteristics become so general that we can barely comprehend them. So, when Whitehead is talking about the metaphysical necessities of extensive connection, he is talking about form in general. No reference is made to the special asymmetry of time or to the creative advance at this level of analysis because he is investigating levels of order that transcend, yet apply throughout all cosmic epochs. Indeed, the peculiarity of this scheme is that it can be thought of without reference to physical time, space, and the creative advance. But this does not mean that it is disconnected. As Whitehead says: "The 'extensive' scheme is nothing else than the generic morphology of the internal relations which bind the actual occasions into a nexus, and which bind the prehensions of any one actual occasion into a unity, coordinately divisible."[55] It is the most general system of relatedness of all possibilities, but only as a system limited by its relevance to the general fact of actuality.

So the idea of a continuum is a spatialization, or an abstraction that omits the process by which an individual event comes into being. This is why Whitehead says: "The notion of nature as an organic extensive community omits the equally essential point of view that nature is never complete."[56]

What we must keep in mind is that, for Whitehead, the whole universe evolves from the bottom up. With the becoming and perishing of actual occasions, and the evolution and decay of 'societies' that occur over longer periods of time, cosmic epochs also become and perish over stretches beyond our comprehension. And even beyond cosmic epochs there must be some sense of evolution though the changes may be very minute. The point is that with the passing moment the whole world conspires to produce a new creation and thus changes are felt throughout the universe. This is why Whitehead says that none of the laws of nature give the slightest evidence of necessity.[57] With the running down of a cosmic epoch there is a general decay of the dominant patterns of prehensions constituting these laws. Such laws fade into unimportance once the epoch passes into the background of the past. But as a cosmic epoch passes away and another becomes from an aboriginal disorder of actual occasions, we must conjecture that changes are felt at the higher levels of 'society', even though they may be of negligible importance.

Logical, mathematical, and geometrical laws are usually held in such high epistemological esteem because they are seen as eternally true, or true in all possible worlds. But, for Whitehead, even these laws are not metaphysical truths.[58] They appear to be necessarily true since they are largely unaffected by the process of the lower levels. But it is possible that in some distant cosmic epoch, where there will have been sufficient change in the wider societies, that one plus one will not make the sum of two, *modus ponens* will be an invalid form, and a line will be something other than a breadthless length. This is a genuine possibility if process is the ultimate metaphysical necessity. It is only that the sense of endurance in the ultimate 'societies' is so general and stable that the laws seem eternal, but, in fact, they are only propositions that hold in these levels of social order.

According to the ontological principle, the whole universe is composed of actual occasions whose essence is process. When we abstract from this process of occasions, certain formal properties of extensive connection can be formulated. And as Whitehead says, the relation of whole and part is probably a metaphysical ultimate. Points, lines, surfaces, straightness, and flatness are the geometrical elements applicable to this stage of cosmic history, then there are the more special characteristics of the specific cosmic epoch in question. In ours, the laws of electromagnetic phenomena reign. In others, perhaps laws of antielectromagnetic phenomena are dominant, or the social order is radically different from the order we experience. But it is quite clear that nothing of this scheme gains any meaning without the activity of actual occasions.

For Whitehead, we saw that the level of social order known as "pure extension" was the largest conceivable level, but this vastly general 'society' was not the end of relations in the Bradleian sense. There is no final or perfect level of order in the universe. There is always room for improvement, and equally, every chance of destruction. Whitehead therefore criticizes Bradley in several places for absorbing process into the perfection of the Absolute.[59] And, generally speaking, he writes of absolute idealism:

> the immensity of the world negatives the belief that any state of order can be so established that beyond it there can be no progress. This belief in a final order, popular in religious and philosophic thought, seems to be due to the prevalent fallacy that all types of seriality necessarily involve terminal instances.[60]

Clearly Whitehead is allowing for some further order to be achieved out of the nebulous disorder beyond. So, extensive relations must be potentially infinite in both the temporal sense of before and after, and the spatial sense of whole and part. Aside from these most general properties of the extensive continuum, there is no eternal static order as one final container. Just as various forms of seriality extend infinitely in one or both directions, there is no reason why the universe cannot be conceived in similar fashion.

Whitehead could very well accept Bradley's general conclusion that there cannot be individuals or relations without there being some larger whole, but there is no reason to accept one final Whole, if the wholes are themselves generated by the creative process. Instead of postulating one final Whole in order to understand how the levels of society nest inside one another, the essential notion for event-pluralism is that the actual occasion is "the whole universe in process of attainment of a particular satisfaction."[61] The actuality of the universe is derivative from the solidarity in each occasion. This is, I think, what Whitehead means when he says that his cosmology is a "transformation of some of the main doctrines of Absolute Idealism onto a realistic basis." The essential modification is that the "realistic basis" is evolutionary.

Recalling that Whitehead's pluralism necessitates an inversion of Bradley's doctrine of actuality, W. E. Hocking, recording his recollection of a conversation with Whitehead, quotes him as saying:

> I am very near to absolute idealism when you take the finite as an abstraction; the slightest push would push me over. But where I differ is, your Absolute is a super-reality. My point is, when you try to get at a ground of reality more real than the given, you get an abstraction; your super-reality is an under-reality. Reality is always emergence into a finite modal entity.[63]

This may seem odd indeed when we consider Bradley's claim that the Absolute is the most concrete Reality, but of course the Absolute is not the *given* concrete reality but rather a hypothesis about how all the finite centres form one larger concrete Whole. Even Bradley is quite clear that it is only in 'feeling' that we have a low and imperfect example of an immediate whole, and this is never more than the unity of our own finite centre.

So, in the end, as to our central problem of whether the Absolute swallows process in one timeless eternity, or process and the general flux of the creative advance dissolve any conception of a final order, we have opted for Whitehead's position over Bradley's. But in this section, our main aim has been to expose their very different conceptions of the universe.

It may indeed be said that one side reduces time to space by defining all temporal relations in terms of parts or appearances of the Whole, while the other side reduces space to time by defining all spatial relations in terms of process and evolution. In one sense this is fairly accurate, but it is much too simple a formulation to capture the conflict between Bradley and Whitehead. Whether we are monists or pluralists largely depends upon the soundness of the general arguments on relations. And, although Bradley's analysis of the relational was for the most part rejected, we now turn to a more detailed examination of his arguments respecting time, where the problem of relations once again becomes acute.

CHAPTER 6

Time

In this chapter, I concentrate on special problems of time that arise in connection with the conflict between Bradley's conception of the Absolute and Whitehead's notion of the universe as an infinite process. After considering how Whitehead might have attempted to solve various problems raised by Bradley, I shall consider how Santayana's theory of time might be used to articulate more clearly specific arguments for an eternalistic conception of time. Given this new formulation of the position, various objections will be raised in connection with Whitehead's theory of prehension and objectification, and finally I will attempt to defend Whitehead against these objections.

TEMPORAL UNITY AND DIRECTION

Although Bradley never mitigates the severity of his treatment of time as a relatively low appearance on the scale of reality, he does wish to establish "how by its inconsistency time directs us beyond itself."[1] By this we are meant to understand that time must find its wider harmony and consumption within the experience of the Absolute. To this end, Bradley repeatedly argues that the essential cohesion of the universe is a result of the total interdependence of experience happening in an eternal present. Such a teleology does not involve a dependence of becoming in time and satisfaction of purpose in sequential order, but rather the telos of parts that form a de facto whole. From this it is clear that, given its relational and atomistic character as conceived by ordinary thought, time cannot hold a primary place in such a system. It is but an isolated aspect that loses its special character when absorbed into the timelessness of the Absolute.

In two previous chapters, I gave considerable attention to Bradley's views regarding the inconsistency of time as a plurality

131

of discrete moments.[2] But we now turn our attention to the arguments where his theory of the transcendence of time comes clearly into focus. Here the attack is focused on temporal unity and direction as a one-way succession in which everything in the universe must conform.

As regards the unity of time, Bradley says we have a tendency to regard all events "as members in one temporal whole, and standing therefore throughout to one another in relations of 'before' and 'after' or 'together'."[3] However, Bradley regards the possibility of a number of independent time-series as counterevidence for this claim. This, presumably, would look like layers of overlapping series where no one series would be dominant or play the foundational role upon which the others are interwoven. Each would have its own phenomenal order. To illustrate these independent series, Bradley considers dreams, imaginative wanderings, and fictions. Each dream, for example, has its own logical order and time lapse, yet when considered in relation to the order in a different dream or fiction, we find no sense in which they can be said to be part of one series of real events. This, Bradley concludes, leads us "to realize that the successive need have no temporal connection."[4]

On a slightly different but related theme, Bradley now considers direction in time which follows much the same course as temporal unity. The direction of time poses a most interesting problem: Does time move forward into a novel future, or do events, becoming as fresh sensations in the present, immediately slip backwards into the past? Though Bradley thinks the latter is more natural, either direction is entirely dependent on the psychological state and present interests of the perceiver.[5] Why one may be preferred to another is not a matter of how time is directed in Reality but, rather, is based on the practical outlook of animal nature. Mockingly, he relates such sense of direction in time to the principle by which fish feed heading upstream instead of downstream.[6] Since temporal direction is simply a construction of the perceiver, it must be seen as a convenient way of dealing with our world.

In *Appearance and Reality*, Bradley entertains the possibility of a variety of time-series existing in the Absolute, one of which is the exact reversal our order of events. In such a world we may conceive of a technologically advanced society deevolving into unicellular organisms. By our understanding, "Death would come before birth, the blow would follow the wound, and all must seem irrational."[7] One is reminded of the story of Benjamin Button in F. Scott Fitzgerald's *Tales of the Jazz Age*.[8] Moving backwards from grave to cradle, Benjamin's life began in the last stage of senility and thereafter aged in reverse until he perished as an embryo, splitting into an egg and a sperm. Bradley's main aim in this conceptual experiment is to show that there is no logical objection to the possibility of other time-series that are completely independent of the one we experience. If there are multiple overlapping directions in time that run counter to the one of our own experience, then our own sense of direction holds no special significance in reality, and in the timeless perfection of the Absolute, all times must be transmuted into an eternal present.

Bradley again takes up the problem of direction in time in his essay, "Why Do We Remember Forwards And Not Backwards?" As the title suggests, his main concern is the general tendency of memory to trace events forward from the past to present.[9] In his analysis, however, he wishes to refute the idea that memory follows a real direction in time. The image of a flowing stream is used to indicate the direction of our consciousness in time. Bradley explains using an example where *a* refers to an identity among change in a succession of events, *abc-acd-ade-aef-afg-*:

> It is not a stream in general which we have to do with, but the stream of *our* events. And here we have the essence. It is our psychical states which furnish both the flood and all the matter which flows or which stands against the stream. In the succession of these states it is the group of self, more or less unvarying, that has the place taken by *a* in our scheme. And it is the attitude of this group towards the incoming new presentations on which everything turns. It is this relation which gives a meaning to *direction*, and shows the essence of our problem.[10]

The forward direction of time, Bradley thinks, is tied to our tendency in thinking that consciousness flows as a stream forwards to "meet fresh experiences." Or, if we think of time as moving backwards "it is because we do not go back," but hold our own against change, like the fish feeding upstream. Lastly, if we think of ourselves as stationary, the direction is relative to our experience and makes no *real* difference. In the end, Bradley thinks that our tendency to remember forwards is tied with the first of these notions of direction in time. It is simply a habit, in that we anticipate the future, and this suits our needs best for approaching coming sensations and actions. Instances in which we would remember backwards are just as accurate, but not so common, because we would be directed away in time from our present selves, which concern us most.[11] This, Bradley concludes, should convince us that direction is just as much an illusion as time itself. The appearance of a direction that time follows is of our own psychological making and not part of the nature of reality.

The contrast between Bradley and Whitehead on these issues could not be more sharp. Whitehead must therefore challenge Bradley from the point of view that our intuitive grasp of time as moving forward exemplifies the very process of becoming in which the antecedent world forces a novel moment in the immediate present. This asymmetry of concrete relations implies a concept of time in which the past is determinate, the present in the making and the future indeterminate. There is no altering what is fixed in the past but, as such data exist as an accumulation in the present, there is a genuine choice to be made regarding the future. As the present moment sheds its actuality it does not merely become nothing as it fades into the past. Having perished, its determinate and individual character is preserved in the present, though its degree of preservation is dependent upon the positive prehensions of present and future occasions. The process of time is not, therefore, an illusion or a shifting of eternally present occasions of experience, but rather the actualization of a potential as each occasion achieves a new particular and then experiences a subsequent loss of actuality.

The ultimate view underlying Bradley's attacks on temporal unity and direction is a universe of symmetrical interdependence. His realms of possible time-series do not, however, refute or show the absurdity of time as one unifying process of events. First, it is highly unlikely that the fictions and dreams that Bradley regards as having their own independent time-series occur to any of us as having the same degree of reality as our normal conscious states.

We can surely discriminate by the fact that dreams and unconscious states do not form a continuous identity of the self, as is the case with normal consciousness. Second, his attempt to refute the idea of one asymmetrical series of temporal unity is based on the erroneous assumption that these realms of floating fictions are completely independent of the temporal process. But our experience of dreams, imaginative wanderings, and various fictions do happen within the context of one dominant temporal succession, and the mode of being that they have is entirely dependent upon our memory of them.[12] Bradley does not give this sufficient attention. What he does ask us to consider is how various fictions and dreams stand in the order of before and after in time.[13] Each fictional series, he thinks, has its own logical order, but is independent, insofar as we try to relate it to one temporal process. It must be noted, however, that each came into existence by our creating them in time. Upon subsequent reflection, each fiction easily has the appearance of not being a part of time, especially when considered in relation to one another. Thus, their status seems equal to that of timeless universals. But unlike the universal, the fiction is dependent upon memory in the temporal process.

Let us pursue an example to clarify the point. When Mozart wrote the score for his *Don Giovanni*, his act of creating the opera was in the temporal process, and each time it was subsequently performed it had a phenomenal unity recognized as *Don Giovanni*. The individual notes that constitute the music of the opera exist as timeless universals, however the patterns of musical notes and lyrics themselves are not universals. They were created at some definite point in history and can be destroyed or lost to humanity at some future point. Hence the opera does not occupy an independent realm with its own time. In Whitehead's view, it exists only insofar as actual occasions prehend this pattern or sequence of eternal objects. The only sense in which *Don Giovanni* exists after its composition and aside from its being performed, is in some form of memory (e.g., musical notation, or human memory) which has potential to be performed in the present. Accordingly, patterns of universals or eternal objects would not establish the existence of a number of time-series.

Following this line of thought, the argument opposing direction, though parasitic on the argument opposing temporal connection, can be seen as clarifying Bradley's position regarding symmetry. The direction of a series that we experience as $a,b,c,d, \ldots z$ is counterbalanced and therefore neutralized in a totality that contains the world in which direction runs $z,y,x,w, \ldots a$. Even though Bradley has in mind a multitide of overlapping time-series, for our present purpose it will be sufficient to consider the case running directly opposite to our own experienced world. Bradley asks if such a world is contradictory or anything but possible. But what is crucial about this conceptual experiment is that the reversed direction is not part of our experience, which is directional in terms of aim and memory. It merely occurs as one of many within the comprehensive experience of the Absolute. This being the case, it is conceivable that such a world might exist outside our current cosmic epoch, provided that we are mere observers, and not agents that affect the order of events. Also, with this reversed direction, it must be noted that experience in this world too is an asymmetrical relation; one-way, except from effects to causes. An apple would then roll along the ground, bounce and leap upwards attaching itself to a branch of a tree. A man's life would proceed in the reverse from death to birth, and in such a world people would use *before* and *after* in a sense that would have meanings opposite those we assign them. But what does this all come to? Here we would have a world in which the laws of physics and biology would be reversed to apply to the reversed order in which physical bodies move. Also, the laws of psychology would explain how events are contained in memory and become more vivid until they happen and become a desire or aim, finally vanishing as the bud of an idea. This being so, the creatures in this world would still experience events as an irreversible asymmetric process. Now it seems difficult to see how Bradley establishes the symmetrical case. This world could be reconciled just as easily with the direction of our world. The sequences, $a,b,c,d, \ldots z$ and $z,y,x,w, \ldots a$ would run counter to each other in terms of content, but they would nonetheless be synchronized in one asymmetric process.

What is surely rejected by the primacy of process is the notion that the future can exist as determinate moments beyond the present. That is, a cannot exist as a determinate occasion happening first in one sequence and last in the other. In the reversed order, all that exists at the instance of *a*'s becoming is the becoming of *z*. Bradley, in order to establish the symmetrical case must always presuppose the existence of the Absolute to provide a basis in which events would run counter to one another in separate times. For example, he assumes that all moments in the independent series exist in a timeless Whole. However, without this unnecessary hypothesis, time and direction conform as a one-way dependence.

As active participants in the creative process, that is, as agents that affect the content in experience through our volition, we shape the present and essentially contribute to the direction in time. Anticipation of fresh sensations, then, does describe the nature of directed experience in the sense that we are conscious of creating the present yet equally aware of how that experience will be continuous with the future. That is, the present anticipates existence beyond itself in that its achievement will have value for the future. Without anticipation of the future, "the present collapses, emptied of its proper content."[14]

Though Bradley's theory is founded upon a universe of innumerable centres of experience, he argues that much of our understanding of this experience is illusory. But, if the occasions of experience that compose our psychical states provide a sense of direction as a stream of events moving forward, then why should this not be paradigmatic of the nature of reality? Bradley certainly stresses the importance of our accepting 'feeling' and direct intuition just as it comes without the mutilation of analysis. Yet his interpretation of this experience is fundamentally influenced by the permanent and essentially static conception of the Absolute.

THE ETERNALISTIC THEORY OF TIME

The notion that temporal passage must be resolved ultimately into a static eternity is by no means a novel idea to metaphysicians. Plato argued in the *Timaeus* that time is the "moving image of eternity" and that the common practice of attributing movement and transition to ultimate reality is mistaken. As Plato made the case for his own version of the eternalistic theory, he argued that time is an imperfect mirroring of the selfsameness of eternity. The perfect unity of being takes on a characteristic form in the sensible as a uniform flow.[15]

Bradley's view comes remarkably close to Plato, especially where he argues that Reality does not exist in time but only appears there. But aside from the claims of various forms of idealism, other philosophers who have contemplated the nature of time have discovered something very peculiar about the notion of becoming and perishing and about the unequal ontological status of the past, present, and future. George Santayana, for instance, argues that the basis for the truth of our judgments about the past or future lies in the correspondence between such judgments in the present and the actual existence of past and future events. This leads him to the view that all events are intrinsically present and that past and future are simply relative to the *now* in question. Truth, in Santayana's view, is therefore eternal, but this does not mean that the actual passage of events is resolved into a static eternity. Santayana, in fact, stresses that it is of the very essence of each event, or 'natural moment' to be lapsing into the next. The dynamics of process are not, in his view, illusory, for this too is a part of the eternal truth of things. But the important point to keep in mind is that each moment, though propulsive in one respect, is also eternally fixed in its place in the temporal flux.[16]

Although we shall return to consider the arguments for this theory in more detail later in this section, we must first examine Bradley's theory. Having briefly introduced the central problem which gives rise to what is sometimes called "the eternalistic theory of time," we shall find some indication that Bradley himself leaned in this direction, but of course developed his view in a much more monistic fashion.[17]

At times, Bradley seems to deny that there is a real past or future. He calls such mental phenomena "ideal constructions." The past, for instance, is constructed from the present because it is not directly experienced and must therefore be unreal. Since the past is not a part of immediate experience, it can only be considered in terms of synthetic judgments of sense which involve an inference from our present memory-experience. Similarly, the future would be a construction based on a present expectation.

Reality then can never be known in its totality though our best intuition comes in the undivided immediacy of feeling. As Bradley argues in *The Principles of Logic*: "It is impossible, perhaps, to get directly at reality, except in the content of one presentation; we may never see it, so to speak, but through a hole."[18] Such remarks might lead one to believe that Bradley is advocating the view sometimes called "the philosophy of the present"— in which past and future are unreal because all that truly exists is the particular now immediately present. But this is clearly not the case, for even though Bradley here, and in other places, emphasizes that past and future are, from our point of view, "ideally constructed," he also says they must be real for there to be anything for our judgments to be true about. For example, in his essay, "What is the Real Julius Caesar?" he writes:

> The past and future vary, and they have to vary, with the changes of the present, and, to any man whose eyes are open, such variation is no mere theory but is plain fact. But, though ideal, the past and future are also real, and, if they were otherwise, they could be nothing for judgment or knowledge. They are actual, but must remain incomplete essentially.[19]

But here we seem to be faced with the problem of how the past and future can be both real and ideal. Put another way, how can past and future be actual if time itself remains essentially unreal? Bradley is far from clear about the exact formulation of his theory, but at least here he seems to have approached the idea that all events—past, present and future—are eternally present in the Absolute.

It seems that the obscurity in Bradley's view is due to a tension in his thought between Reality as one timeless moment and reality as many "related" moments contained in this eternal present. The obvious difficulty with the pluralistic conception is the amount of abstraction involved once analysis has cut into the continuous Whole present in immediate 'feeling'. The division of time into a continuum of past, present, and future events leads invariably to an infinity of relations, and this is never ultimately satisfactory in Bradley's view. However we must also keep in mind that some of the restrictions of Bradley's radical monism are mitigated by his notion of degrees of truth and reality, and this I take to be the key to understanding his view.

As we recall, Bradley's overall metaphysical position involves several levels of truth and reality that are adequate for their specified purposes. Hence, various types of thought that deal with some form of plurality are necessary and this is particularly true of our judgments about past and future events. Once the Absolute is broken down into various degrees of reality, we discover a hierarchy of levels in which these various forms of plurality begin to appear.

For our present purposes we distinguish four levels, and, once again, we employ the distinction made earlier between enduring and momentary centres of experience.[20] Our analysis of this hierarchy proceeds from the most unified to the most divided:

1. The Absolute as an undivided Individual;
2. The Absolute as the unity of enduring centres;
3. The enduring centres as the unity of momentary centres;
4. The momentary centres as the unity of "that" and "what."

At the first level, the Absolute is the only fully complete and final Reality existing in one timeless eternal present. Then, one step down, the Absolute is the unity of an indefinite number of enduring centres of experience. Since they are at one with the Absolute they are eternal, though, from our perspective, they endure throughout all time. Then, another step down, each enduring centre is the unity of its many momentary qualifications, which are the momentary centres, or 'this-nows.' As Bradley says on this point, the enduring centre "contains a lapse and a before and after, but these are subordinate."[21] It is at this level that time appears and judgment about the various moments of time becomes important. And, finally, another step down, we arrive at the level in which each momentary centre is a unity of existence and content, of "that" and "what" fused together to make up the individual psychical unities.

Now quite clearly, each lower level will be an adjective of the immediately higher level, and each will therefore have a perfectly determinate place in the Absolute. All will be present, but at the third and fourth levels, past and future will be relative to the point of view of any particular now of a momentary centre. That is, each this-now will feel its place in the particular series of the enduring centre to which it belongs, and it will also have a certain perspective on the Whole from this particular place.

What we must remember is that Reality, for Bradley, is continuous throughout, but since our given presentation is merely a restricted hole through which we gaze into the eternal, we see it only partially. This is why past and future are but constructions from our present point of view. We ideally fill in the portions of the continuous reality that are not present. But for the Absolute, past and future are just as real and actual as is our given present. All moments, then, are just eternally present in the Absolute, even though they remain essentially incomplete and imperfect in themselves.

Bradley himself does not say this in so many words, but I think this is the upshot of his theory, and it is the only sense which I can make of his notion that past and future are both ideal and real. That is, what makes our judgments more or less true or false is that there is that portion of reality actually present in the Absolute experience, even though ultimately any judgment distorts what is given to our experience.

One point emphasized by many absolute idealists is that any representation of the Absolute will fail miserably simply because our humble, finite perspective on Reality never comes close to grasping the whole of eternity beyond. Also, any particular model will be illuminating only for certain points and wholly inadequate for others. But, if we are to choose the best of the worst, perhaps a sphere comes closest to satisfying this need of an image, and this will aid us in our present discussion. With such a model we can imagine a whole that contains at its core the enduring centres of experience all fused together in absolute harmony, but on the outer surface there are innumerable routes that belong to one centre or another. Such routes will be the various appearances of finite centres in time forming what might be called "space-time worms," and at each point, there will be a momentary centre that fills that portion of reality. Leaving aside for the moment the complications of points of contact where two or more routes cross or run parallel to one another, we can easily conceive of how each momentary centre must always be eternally present from the point of view of the Absolute.

What Bradley seems to say in this connection is that all finite centres of experience are ultimately present and influence one another in some degree or other, but within certain limits we separate them into distinct periods of time that are not contemporary.[22] As he puts this point in the conclusion of his essay on Julius Caesar:

> The real individual then (we find) does not fall merely within a moment, nor is he bounded by his birth and death, nor is he in principle confined to any limited period. He lives *there* wherever the past or future of our 'real' order is present to his mind, and where in any other way whatever he influences or acts on it.[23]

So at the core of Reality lies the real Julius Caesar who was and always will be present there. But what Bradley also says here is that the limits in which we fix the period of Caesar's life (100–44 B.C.) are arbitrary. Thus, there is reason to believe that in the end, Bradley himself would not wholly subscribe to the theory we have constructed above (that all moments are determinately fixed in the Absolute experience) since he does not give too much emphasis to what we have called "momentary centres." Since he thinks the more pluralistic and atomistic views are largely our constructions in order to deal with time, we cannot be sure exactly how such momentary aspects are ordered in the Absolute. But let us return to Santayana, who did expound a pluralistic theory compatible with eternalism, and whose arguments can be used to clarify the more obscure points in Bradley, at least where he seems to have leaned towards some theory of determinationism.

What Santayana calls his "realm of truth" is, in many ways, quite consistent with the Bradleian Absolute. For instance, Santayana says that:

> The truth . . . forms an ideal realm of being impersonal and super-existential. Though everything in the panorama of history be temporal, the panorama itself is dateless: for evidently the sum and system of events cannot be one of them. It cannot occur after anything else. Thus the truth of existence differs altogether in ontological quality from existence itself.[24]

Such views accord quite well with the Bradleain view of the Absolute as the one Reality that has no history but contains histories without end. The realm of truth, like the Absolute, is ontologically distinct and supertemporal; it does not however carry any implications of absolute spirit nor is it the nonrelational One by which everything is finally absorbed. But such differences need not concern us now.[25]

What is quite relevant in this context is that past, present, and future are, for Santayana, eternally fixed in the universe as determinate moments of temporal order. Contrary to Bradley then, Santayana would accept the notion that the reality of Caesar is bounded by his birth and death, but this stretch of history is always present in its own time. The limits of his life are not arbitrary; each moment forms a determinate piece of reality.

As mentioned above, Santayana's central argument for this view is that a judgment must have an existing object, and this applies regardless of the specific period of time that contains the referent. Intelligence, he says, comes to perceive a certain continuity of events and definite truths about them.[26] For instance, in our own flow of consciousness we have a direct experience of the truth of each moment and of the substantial derivation of one to the next. But the truth of each moment is a fact that does not itself change with the passage of time.

Santayana insists that the present point of view, the I or now of present immediacy, is particularly deceptive with regard to the eternal truth of all time. Since "nowness runs like a fire along the fuse of time"[27] we might be led to see truth changing as fast as the spark of immediacy. But, for him, this is to confuse the essence now with particular nows. Particular nows change one for another in rapid succession, but the truth of each distinct now in its determinate place in the flux forms the unchangeable truth of history. The error in thinking that past events have simply perished is therefore a result of sliding "from a truism to a private perspective." That Caesar lived long ago is true only in relation to *our* present. But Caesar's present is a truth that does not change: it is always there in that particular portion of reality.

In Santayana's view, then, time does not slip away, or to use Locke's phrase, "perpetually perish." Judgments about the past are true or false because each event is itself present and only past or future in relation to the event that happens to be illuminated as *our* present. In what must be the clearest statement of this argument, Santayana writes:

> If Julius Caesar was alive at a certain date, it was then true, it had been true before, and it will be true always that at that date he was or would be or had been alive. These three assertions, in their deliverance, are identical; and in order to be identical in their deliverance, they have to be different in form, because the report is made in each case from a different point in time, so that the temporal perspectives of the same fact, Caesar's death on the Ides of March, require different tenses of the verbs. This is a proof of the instability of knowledge in contrast to the fixity of truth. For the whispered oracle, *Beware the Ides of March*, the tragic event was future; for the Senators crowding round Pompey's statue it was present; for the historian it is past: and the truth of these several perspectives, each from its own point of origin, is a part of the eternal truth about that event.[28]

So the pain that Caesar felt the moment he was stabbed with three and twenty wounds does not fade because it occurred over two thousand years ago; it was, is, and always will be present in that portion of reality.

From this it is quite clear that past, present, and future must all have an equal ontological status, regardless of which particular date we choose as our point of departure. The future beyond my writing this sentence is just as determinate in character as is yesterday or the day of Caesar's death. It is only that our knowledge of such future events is limited by the fact that they have not occurred in relation to our present, and this is, Santayana claims, only a peculiarity of human life—that we have much knowledge of the past and little of the future. But the alleged disparity between past and future is not an issue of our knowledge that wants to identify truth with our knowledge of it. Eternal truth is, rather, supertemporal and involves no limitation of scope in which human opinions operate. It is complete, accurate and perfectly determinate in either direction.

REPLIES TO SOME OBJECTIONS TO WHITEHEAD

Our discussion has now reached the threshold of our final comparison, yet at the same time we seem to be confronted with a grave difficulty. In one respect, the central issue raised by the eternalistic theory of time is crucial to Whitehead's final question: "What does it all come to?" For without some fadeless preservation of the perfect moment there can be no determinate truth.[29] The passing of each moment cannot simply become nothing. If it did, the position would not be altogether different from the Heraclitean paradox of "that which is always becoming and never is." The basic problem for a philosophy of process, then, is how novelty does not entail loss, for the flux of existence is essentially meaningless without reference to permanence. As Whitehead on this point often quoted:

> Abide with me;
> Fast falls the eventide.[30]

But on the other hand, the position we have sketched above is clearly at odds with Whitehead regarding the equal ontological status of past, present, and future. If indeed Santayana's argument is a sound one, creativity cannot be the ultimate principle governing the becoming of experience, for the truth of every actual occasion is definite prior to its instant of becoming.

In this connection, Timothy Sprigge, a proponent of Santayana's theory of time, has in *The Vindication of Absolute Idealism* and elsewhere, raised several pointed objections to Whitehead's theory of prehension and objectification.[31] Since these two notions are crucial to the mechanism of process, the criticisms advanced by Sprigge are important in order to clarify the contrast with the theory of eternalism. And although I cannot, in this limited space, do justice to his intricate arguments for "holistic relations" essential to his view, I will simply point to various ways in which the process view might be defended against these objections.

Sprigge concedes that in large measure the ontology of actual occasions accords quite well with his own conclusions, but he rejects the notion of a later occasion containing an earlier one as opposed to some manner of echoing it. If an actual occasion has been prehended by a later one, it has lost subjective immediacy, or, as Sprigge puts it, "suffered a kind of sea-change" and attained objective immortality.[32] But he asks, how can this earlier occasion be the same particular as an element in the later one?[33]

Whitehead's crucial point is that an actual occasion creates itself out of its causes; it prehends the multitude of occasions in its immediate past from which it forms its novel synthesis, and then is broken down into data for future prehensions. But it is clear that in this process a past occasion does not survive as a whole in any future occasions. It has only a partial existence (with a continuance of subjective form) in a multitude of subsequent occasions. The very concept of prehension demands that a successor eliminate certain elements incompatible with its own unique subjective aim. But if a past occasion has been altered such that it exists only as separate elements objectified in many present ones, what guarantees the truth of it when it was subjectively immediate? Why should not the death of Julius Caesar become a little less bloody as subsequent prehensions thousands of years later continue to redistribute the data that was this determinate event in the history of the Roman empire? The upshot of Whitehead's theory, at this point, seems to force him to the unfortunate conclusion that there is nothing actual that would settle the issue of what would make a judgment about the inherent character of this event true.

In effect, Sprigge argues that the whole notion of perishing or loss of subjective immediacy is incoherent and that we must accept the idea that Caesar's death is an untransformed event, eternally present in that particular portion of Reality.

Sprigge's objection to Whitehead really falls into two separate problems that we shall address as follows: (i) the problem of prehension, and (ii) the problem of perishing. Both are, of course, intimately connected in order to understand the mechanism of process, but for our present purpose, we shall approach them separately.

(i) As to the first problem, in which Sprigge asks how an earlier occasion that has lost subjective immediacy can be the same particular as an element in the later one (or ones), we deny this. The conjunctive unity achieved at the end point of its process is not the same *particular* as the disjunctive diversity scattered among its successors. That is, the elements or objects prehended as data are not to be understood as the real particulars of the process. Only the actual occasions achieve this ontological status once they have become fully determinate and complete moments of experience. Also, it is quite clear that we can make no sense of prehension of the past without the crucial point that when an occasion is subjectively immediate, the extensive characteristics and the objects have not yet appeared. Objects only arise once the occasion has reached its satisfaction and has become a determinate entity. The whole notion of subjective immediacy means that the occasion is still in the making and therefore indeterminate. But once it does reach its satisfaction, the truth of this entity is not altered by the fact that the successors must work with something. Since the successors cannot create *ex nihilo*, there must be some material or data there to manipulate in order to produce the novel unity.

Some explanation is still needed. What we require is more elucidation of the various stages of the concrescence where the fluency of the past world makes its transition into the actual world of the immediate present.

Generally speaking, the occasion must be seen as a process that moves from *becoming*, in which the occasion is subjectively immediate, to *being*, which is the completed satisfaction or superject, to *perishing*. It is this second stage in which the determinate entity appears and becomes a potential object for a novel becoming. When an occasion reaches its satisfaction and becomes part of the actual world composed of other occasions that have reached their end points simultaneously, it becomes a datum for a successor now in the stage of becoming (i.e., subjective immediacy). But this new occasion, having picked up where the others left off, begins to break down the actual world to form its own conjunctive unity and will choose only those elements compatible with its own ideal. This brings us to the crucial point. Even though the chief ontological status of the predecessor is that of an initium of its successors, the organic unity thus formed is greater than the sum of its parts that will become the elements in subsequent prehensions. Hence, any element that survives beyond this organic unity is but an abstraction from this concrete whole.

Sprigge goes further to say that those who hold this view of the objectification of the earlier in the later have the notion of influence as injection by one experience of some part of its quality into a successor, but this is inconceivable unless understood as "the passage of quality from one locus to another within something like a single specious present."[34] But are actual occasions, natural moments, or momentary centres of experience so impenetrable that no 'feelings' of the others can enter into them and affect their own internal constitution? A simple echo or manner of influence does not seem to do the trick. And even here it is hard to make any sense of Santayana's idea of moments "lapsing into one another" without some penetration of content. One's ability to sympathize with the type of experience another being has seems a good point of departure here, especially since this is important for Sprigge's own view.[35] But it becomes rather difficult to imagine how one could truly sympathize with the reality of another being if one did not literally share in her experience, and feel at least some of those 'feelings'. If so much is granted, the door is open for something like Whitehead's concept of prehension because any experience of sympathy that one may feel for another is of that experience in what is one's own immediate past. This is what Whitehead claims is happening in the first stage of becoming in the new occasion, namely, a receptive sympathy. He says: "There is always the vague feeling of things beyond us, which are also within us, and within which we live."[36]

(ii) Now however much we may be inclined to accept the notion of prehension as one experience containing elements of other experiences, we are still left with the problem of perishing. Where is the real past if it is only the elements that survive in the present? This I take to be the stronger part of Sprigge's objection to Whitehead, and it is one that deserves considerable attention.

According to Whitehead, the past is real but gone. Just when the occasion reaches its satisfaction (from becoming to being) it passes on its data to the immediate present and perishes. But where is it, if real and not still actual in the past? As we have said, it is partially here in the present, but as past, it is dead and gone. But if only the constituents survive, what determines the truth of the occasion as it was when present?

In reply to this objection it will be necessary to anticipate many of the conclusions of our final chapter, where Whitehead's notion of the consequent nature of God finds a definite parallel with Bradley's notion of the Absolute. Whitehead himself recognized that the prehension and objectification of finite actualities was not sufficient to complete his final vision of reality.

In the "Final Interpretation" of *Process and Reality*, Whitehead remarks that: "Objectification involves elimination," for the present never fully embodies the past in its totality. The world craves for novelty, yet, at the same time, it "is haunted by terror at the loss of the past."[37] Such is our experience of the joy of birth and the sorrow of death in the world. But the whole issue of the loss of the past sets the stage for the most general formulation of the religious problem. Whitehead writes:

> In the temporal world, it is the empirical fact that process entails loss: the past is present under an abstraction. But there is no reason, of any ultimate metaphysical generality, why this should be the whole story.[38]

Indeed the truth of the temporal world must be somewhere in actuality, and Whitehead's solution here involves one actual entity that moves with the whole of creation, absorbing each occasion in perfect harmony. As he says, "there can be no determinate truth, correlating impartially the partial experiences of many actual entities, apart from one actual entity to which it can be referred."[39] "The truth itself is nothing else than how the composite natures of the organic actualities of the world obtain adequate representation in the divine nature."[40] By one actual entity, Whitehead means the consequent nature of God where every actuality is prehended as a determinate whole.

But granted Whitehead's view at this point, another problem arises. As Sprigge points out in an article appropriately entitled "Ideal Immortality," the attempt to resolve the problem of perishing by envisaging the realm of past events as contained in God's memory of all things that have happened creates another problem of distinguishing the real past event from the memory of it in God's mind.[41] Whitehead's use of the term *representation* in the passage quoted above does indeed suggest that there is such a difference. But he also says that the passing moment can find its adequate intensity only by submission to permanence, which indicates that he thought of the absorption as something more than just a cosmic memory. In a reference to the contrast between Locke and Plato, he writes:

> The perfect realization is not merely the exemplification of what in abstraction is timeless. It does more: it implants timelessness

on what in its essence is passing. The perfect moment is fadeless in the lapse of time. Time has then lost its character of 'perpetual perishing'; it becomes the 'moving image of eternity.'[42]

Let us then see how such an interpretation is possible by applying the concept of prehension to God.

Whitehead says that God is devoid of negative prehensions. He prehends the whole world positively such that he saves it as it passes into his immediacy. God differs from actual occasions of the temporal world in that he is an eternal actual entity that never perishes. As opposed to the orthodox Christian conception, Whitehead's God is dynamic, creating, and flowing with the world, and God therefore changes not into a more excellent being but into a more excellent state of the same being. Through his prehensions, nothing is lost that was a "mere wreckage" in the temporal world.[43] All becomes objectively immortal.

If God positively prehends the whole world, this is not a mere memory in the cosmic mind. When he prehends the world it becomes the internal constitution of his being. Hence, every occasion, once it is absorbed into God's essence, is preserved as perfectly determinate in every aspect. And if this sort of retention justifies the reality of the past and satisfies the problem of the interdependence between the permanent eternal side of the universe and the momentary finite side, the problem as to how we distinguish between the real past and the cosmic mind that retains it vanishes. The nonactuality of the past only refers to the finite character of the temporal world. Objective immortality, when considered as an aspect of God's nature, provides the notion of the eternal presence of all that has happened. This explains why Whitehead says that, apart from God, every actuality is merely a "passing whiff of insignificance."

Perhaps Whitehead's notion of perishing is rather misleading in the sense that it carries with it the implication of "dead and gone," or becoming nothing. It may therefore help if we distinguish two senses of perishing: (i) perishing from the temporal world, and (ii) perishing from reality. Clearly Whitehead does not mean that occasions completely vanish from reality (ii), if, in fact, they "live for evermore" as elements in God's nature. According to the ontological principle, everything must be somewhere in actuality, and Whitehead explicitly says that the principle is maintained by the absorption of finite actualities into the divine nature.[44] On the other hand, Whitehead does mean that an occasion perishes from the temporal flux in order to make room for the new (i).

What I take to be the Whiteheadian modification of the theory of determinationism is that occasions cannot be eternally "subjectively immediate" because this stage of becoming is indeterminate. There cannot be events there in the past world still 'feeling' that particular portion of reality because none of them would be determinate entities. They would all be eternally "frustrated" in the stage of becoming. Thus, it is only as completed entities that something is available for the prehensions of the future occasions, and for God, where adequate intensity is finally obtained.

One negative consequence of this position is that, one way or another, it seems that subjective immediacy is lost. Whitehead would have to accept the notion that the truth of each occasion, as it was when subjectively immediate, is preserved as objectified by God, but only as the determinate choices it made in forming a satisfaction. God knows, in objectifying them, what they were as subjectively immediate by the very character of the final entity that was prehended as a whole.

So, we see that past events must be somewhere in reality for there to be any truth about them. But what about future events? We have not yet addressed the issue of the status of the future in Whitehead's view. For as Santayana argued, if we accept the determinateness of the past, it is relatively easy to see how the equal determinateness of the future follows. If one side is fixed, so is the other. But, on the other hand, if creativity is the ultimate metaphysical principle, as Whitehead and Hartshorne argue, no actual occasion, not even God, has yet reached the future and created anything beyond the immediate past. Hence there is nothing that would make a judgment about a future event true because there is literally nothing there. The point that Whitehead makes in this connection is that: "The proposition 'Caesar crossed the Rubicon' could not be felt by Hannibal in any occasion of his existence on earth."[45] No actual occasion can feel a proposition, if its actual world does not *include* the logical subjects of that proposition.[46] As we recall, the essential point of the argument for equal determination was that there is no real difference between past and future (aside from the present now which establishes point of view) because all events are "intrinsically present." But the determinateness of the present is the crucial issue at stake in order to show the equal determinateness of events on either side, first, from present to past, and then from present and past to future. This is precisely what Whitehead rejects.

From the process point of view, *intrinsically present* essentially means a stage of indeterminateness. Within the duration, or specious present, that constitutes the "subjective immediacy" of an occasion, there is something determinate, but this is only what is felt as already settled by the actual world of the immediate past. The present itself is essentially a transition where the potential objects supplied by this actual world are in the process of actualization, and this is what provides us with a sense of genuine choice regarding our present actions. The present is always a transition of *becoming* determinate. And indeed, this being the case, it follows that the future must be open.

Of course this very rich and complex activity of the immediate present and the whole notion of stages of the concrescence is not likely to be accepted by determination theorists. Sprigge, for example, denies that there is this much going on in any occasion of human experience.[47] But those who espouse the theory of determinationism hold that all genuine possibilities are exhaustively actualized. And this being so, actual occasions would be devoid of value since all of the possibilities must be already fixed in actuality. The problem with this is that it stamps an air of illusion on our experience, and denies the value orientation of subjectivity.

I think there is a sleight of hand in Santayana's argument in that he moves from the truth of the past to the truth of the future, but always in retrospect. The future of the Ides of March is determinate only for those who now have that future in their past. Santayana thus treats all events—past, present, and future—as if they were all past. Perhaps it is no accident that the examples of determinationism work from the present backwards.

Santayana's theory of time also seems quite odd in that it combines equal determination of all events and the genuine asymmetry of the flux in which predecessors lapse into successors, i.e., a one-way influence. But are these two notions satisfactorily combined in his theory? If an event is forever present in its own place in the flux, this would deprive it of its very eventfulness in affecting the course of events beyond its present position. How can an event truly influence any other event if both predecessors and successors are equally determinate? Another question which naturally arises in this context is this: Why do not future events equally influence past ones if the limits are absolutely fixed in both directions? It seems that Santayana is saying that all events are interdependent *and* that dependence works only one way.

What is usually meant when philosophers have claimed that time is unreal is that our intuitive grasp of becoming and perishing is largely illusory. This is because time is interpreted not just as it is experienced, but usually through some sort of transcendental and essentially static realm of being or Absolute. But if all of time is eternally present (as opposed to the eternal presence of the past), this sense of the importance of the present moment, becoming afresh in the flux of experience, loses its special meaning.

According to the process view, the asymmetry from past to present is unique in the sense that it is cumulative. Our present memory-experience of the past provides a good indication of definite traces of it. But what is there in the present that provides any traces of the future? Expectation is a poor example of a future analogue of memory. At most it provides us with probability. For Whitehead the truth is always unfolding. The truth about the past is retrospective while the truth about the future is simply a matter of possibility. Santayana is right to claim that truth does not change. But it does not follow that there is an unchanging truth about the future.

CHAPTER 7

God and the Absolute

UNIVERSAL ABSORPTION

Throughout the course of this essay we have seen considerable resistance on the part of Whitehead to a suprarelational Absolute reality. In the early chapters, I attempted to elucidate definite points of affinity between Bradley and Whitehead with respect to the doctrine of experience, but in the later chapters the interpretation of 'feeling' in terms of a distinctive pluralistic ontology led to conflict under three major topics of investigation: (1) relations, (2) extension, and (3) time. However, as indicated in the last section of our preceding chapter, there is one characteristic of Bradley's Absolute that Whitehead accepts as essential to complete his system of reality.

As we recall, in the preface to *Process and Reality*, Whitehead wrote: "though throughout the main body of the work I am in sharp disagreement with Bradley, the final outcome is after all not so greatly different."[1] And in a very late essay entitled "Process and Reality," Whitehead articulates what he means by the "final outcome":

> If you get a general notion of what is meant by perishing, you will have accomplished an apprehension of what you mean by memory and causality, what you mean when you feel that what we are is of infinite importance, because as we perish we are immortal. That is the one key thought around which the whole development of *Process and Reality* is woven, and in many ways I find that I am in complete agreement with Bradley.[2]

In this final chapter of our comparative analysis, we shall focus our attention on the notion of the universal absorption of all finite actualities in one eternal actual entity. Let us then first look to Bradley for the source of this idea with which Whitehead finds himself in "complete agreement."

One of Bradley's central arguments for the existence of the Absolute focuses on the mere fragmentariness of 'feeling', and

155

our sense of incompleteness and imperfection that comes with the passing of each moment. In *Appearance and Reality*, he argues that the universe, in its diversity, has always shown itself to be inexplicable.[3] But at the same time he thinks that 'feeling' supplies us with a clue as to how the universe finally comes together in absolute perfection. Bradley repeatedly emphasizes that such perfection is never comprehended by man in any detail, but to grasp something of its nature in broad outline is sufficient for the purpose of knowing ultimate Reality.

In 'feeling' we have an immediate experience of a nonrelational many-into-one, which, if developed to a final completion, provides us with a basis for belief in a Whole that is qualified nonrelationally by every fragment of experience.[4] Since 'feeling' supplies us with only a "low and imperfect example of an immediate whole," we are compelled to develop further the many-into-one principle to the idea of a perfect Experience that embraces all finite appearances in absolute harmony.[5] This constitutes satisfaction of the intellect for Bradley. Reality as Absolute is the crowning conception attained by the intellect in its struggle to comprehend the less intelligible forms of appearance and imperfection. Thus he writes:

> The universe as a whole may be called intelligible. It may be known to come together in such a way as to realize, throughout and thoroughly, the complete demands of perfect intellect. And every single element, again, in the world is intelligible because it is taken up into and absorbed in a whole of this character.[6]

Finitude, diversity and appearance can only become intelligible by our realization of how things come together in one final Experience, which, for Bradley, is achieved by nothing short of the Absolute. Everything begins and ends in 'feeling'. The many become One.

Since for Bradley, the Absolute absorbs every detail of finite appearance into a final unity, perfection requires that it transform all diversity and conflict into cosmic harmony. All discord, strife, and opposition must come to rest in one final unity; goodness, evil, beauty, ugliness, pleasure, suffering, and error all come together in a unity that includes all, yet cannot be identified with any one per se.

The idea comes very close to Whitehead's doctrine of transmutation. Whenever diversity and conflict are felt as a harmonious unity, there must be a transmutation of the many once absorbed into the final 'feeling'. As Bradley says: "We have a rearrangement not merely of things but of their internal elements. We have an all-pervasive transfusion with a re-blending of all material."[7] This is essential when we consider how it is possible that opposition and discord finally achieve harmonious unity. In fact, the doctrine of transmutation is exactly what is required in Bradley's philosophy in order that the Absolute override the relational form of ordinary thought. In the process of filtering, diversity in the lower levels is blended and transmuted into a richer and more concrete Whole.

But here a problem arises. Bradley, in several places, is quite insistent on the point that, in the process of absorption by which transmutation takes effect, individual natures are lost.[8] This applies whether we are concerned with selves, finite centres or mere properties of individual facts. Yet, in other places he is equally, if not more strongly, insistent that nothing is lost, and that it is only by realizing how things come together in a larger Whole that we understand how every single appearance survives in the result. He says: "We can find no province of the world so low but the Absolute inhabits it. Nowhere is there even a single fact so fragmentary and so poor that to the universe it does not matter."[9]

So, on the one hand, transmutation and perfection in the final unity seems to demand that the constituent individual natures and appearances surrender their unique characters to the Whole, yet on the other hand, the only sense in which all things finite reach their ultimate immortality in the universe is by consumption in this higher 'Feeling' which at once both retains and transmutes them. This we shall identify as the problem of transmutation. It applies to both Bradley and Whitehead and serves as a final point of comparison.

Bradley is well aware of such an objection to his Absolute. If in the process of absorption all individual detail and variety are completely lost, the end result would indeed be really poorer. The Absolute would be simply a "flat monotony of emptiness" standing outside of all life as a bare Thing-in-itself.[10] But he says this would be a serious misunderstanding of the final solution. Because we cannot tell how inconsistencies are united or how the final unity harmonizes all detail, this does not imply that all detail is abolished. He argues that: "We do not know how all these partial unities come together in the Absolute, but we may be sure that the content of not one is obliterated."[11] And in another place he offers the solution that even though the private characters remain, they must be "neutralized by complement and addition."[12] There must be an attenuated importance of the individual nature in the Whole such that the balance can be achieved, but quite clearly it does not vanish. In fact, Bradley argues that the Absolute is there to see that nothing is lost in the end.[13] But the Whole will always be an infinitely richer Individual than the mere sum of its parts.

By and large, when Bradley is concerned with loss of individual natures he means the sense of absolute independence must be lost once we accept the idea that inconsistency and imperfection can only be resolved by a more complete and comprehensive form of Reality. Individuals and private characters do exist though none exist in and by themselves. In fact, for Bradley, it is only by absorption in the higher Reality that the individual has gained its survival beyond its merely finite and transitory character. As he sums up his position with a mastery of eloquence, he writes:

> 'For love and beauty delight', it is no matter where they have shown themselves, 'there is no death nor change'; and this conclusion is true. These things do not die, since the Paradise in which they bloom is immortal. That Paradise is no special region nor any given particular spot in time and space. It is here, it is everywhere where any finite being is lifted into that higher life which alone is waking reality.[14]

There is, however, one qualification that remains in the end. Even though the Absolute becomes richer through absorbing every detail of individual appearance, it is clear that some appearances are more real than others. So, for example, since Bradley thinks that beauty and goodness contain more reality than ugliness and evil, the end result must be understood as balanced only in the sense in which the appearances find their proper place in the eternal hierarchy.

THE CONSEQUENT NATURE OF GOD

When Whitehead claims that he is in complete agreement with Bradley, or that the final outcome of his cosmology is not so greatly different, it is clear that he has in mind the ultimate immortality of the temporal world as it passes into God's nature. For Whitehead, the concept of universal absorption of the finite into one eternal harmony supplied the key to the problem of how the two cravings of the world could be jointly satisfied—that permanence and transience could be combined in such a way that novelty does not mean loss. Although it is clear that Whitehead has overstated his agreement with Bradley, we shall find that his conception of the consequent nature of God does have strong points of contact with the Bradleian Absolute. Where his concept of God differs, however, we shall find that he has serious problems that do not arise for a monist such as Bradley. But before we pursue these problems, let us first concentrate on the points of affinity with Bradley.

The principle of harmony of opposites is fundamental to Whitehead's thought. In his view, the universe has a side that is mental and permanent, and a side that is physical and transient. He says: "The key to metaphysics is this doctrine of mutual immanence, each side lending to the other a factor necessary for its reality."[15] Much of this becomes clear in his natural theology where God is understood to embody this harmony of opposites in himself. He* is the reason for order and provides the transition from the eternal to the actual, and the actual to the eternal. Like the Bradleian Absolute, God is the beginning and the end of 'feeling', the alpha and omega of existence.

Whitehead argues that God is not to be conceived as an exception to the metaphysical principles, but rather as their chief exemplification.[16] Like every actual occasion, God has a twofold nature: one side that is conceptual and atemporal and another side that is physical and temporal. But as one final actual entity,

---

*Although I use the pronoun *he* to refer to Whitehead's God, it is clear that *she* is just as accurate. In this respect, Bradley's impersonal Absolute escapes the difficulty of sexist language and semantic disasters.

God differs from ordinary actual occasions of the temporal world in several important ways.

According to Whitehead, God has a side that is primordial and a side that is consequent. As primordial, God is the aboriginal instance of creativity and the keeper of the wealth of atemporal potentials. He is the primordial conceptual valuation of the entire multiplicity of eternal objects, and, in this respect, he is the beginning of 'feeling' in the world by providing a lure for their realization. For Whitehead, God is therefore immanent in each occasion by supplying it with its initial subjective aim and instilling in it the desire for perfection as is possible in its immediate situation. On the other hand, as consequent, God is the conscious and unbiased reception of the physical world as it passes into the immediacy of his 'feeling'. Regardless of the outcome in the temporal world (i.e., however closely each occasion approximated its ideal for perfection), it is taken into a harmonious unity that preserves every detail of finite achievement. As Whitehead states:

> there is the phase of perfected actuality, in which the many are one everlastingly, without qualification of any loss either of individual identity or of completeness of unity. In everlastingness, immediacy is reconciled with objective immortality.[17]

As consequent, God is therefore the end of 'feeling' in the sense that every occasion of the physical world finds its ultimate completion in a unity that contains it with a fadeless preservation.

So the mental, permanent side of the universe passes into the physical, transient side by the primordial nature of God, which is his guide for realization. The *one* becomes *many* by the unity of God's vision passing into the physical world. And the transient, physical side of the universe passes into the mental, permanent side by the consequent nature of God, which is his coordination of achievement. The *many* become *one* by reaching a final completion and harmonization in God's eternal being.

As we recall from our preceding chapter, it is this conception of God as consequent that finds a definite parallel with the Bradleian Absolute. Bradley, for example, says: "the Absolute is there to see that nothing in the world is lost. That effort which for our vision is wasted, passes over beyond our vision into reality and is crowned with success."[18] Whitehead puts the point in much the same way when he writes:

> [God] saves the world as it passes into the immediacy of his own life. It is the judgement of a tenderness which loses nothing that can be saved. It is also the judgement of a wisdom which uses what in the temporal world is mere wreckage."[19]

On this point, both Bradley and Whitehead agree on the final result—our actions "perish yet live for evermore" as they are perfected by the reality of divine wisdom.

As we recall, the essential concept that brings Bradley and Whitehead together on the notion of universal absorption is to be found in the doctrine of transmutation.[20] The final unity must be achieved by one transmuted 'feeling' where the many become one everlastingly. But here it is obvious that Whitehead runs into the same difficulty as Bradley.

In accordance with Bradley, Whitehead holds that all opposition and discord come together in God's nature such that the immediacies of sufferings, sorrows, failures, triumphs, and joys are "woven by rightness of feeling into the harmony of the universal feeling."[21] But how is it that an individual remains once it has been transmuted into the final unity? In *Modes of Thought*, Whitehead says: "the summation of the many into the one, and the derivation of importance from the one into the many, involves the notion of disorder, of conflict, of frustration."[22] In fact, the very nature of individuality in the physical world involves conflict of finite realizations. But again, how can nothing be lost from this world when everything must be transmuted into one final harmonious 'feeling'?

Although Whitehead makes no explicit reference to the difficulties that arise in connection with the doctrine of transmutation as it specifically applies to God, it is clear that his solution would come fairly close to that of Bradley. Individual facts are not themselves altered once absorbed into the higher unity. Obviously if they were there would be no determinate truth about them. Like Bradley, Whitehead contends that there is no loss of individual identity. The private characters remain, but the synthesis that emerges from this final unification is more than the world as a mere collection of individual achievements. God's consequent nature, Whitehead says: "originates with physical experience derived from the temporal world, and then acquires integration with the primordial side."[23] Or more poetically: "the consequent nature is the weaving of God's physical feelings upon his primordial concepts."[24] So even though every detail of finite fact remains once prehended by God's consequent nature, there is some sense of transformation as the many acquire integration with the all-embracing primordial nature.

The exact meaning of this transformation in God's primordial nature is, at best, unclear. Whitehead emphasizes that this integration of God's twofold nature results in a conscious, infinitely wide harmony of 'feeling' that grows without any loss or fading of its members. Yet in some sense, God, like other actual occasions, necessarily involves a valuation and coordination of his prehensions. This would result in a certain frustration of conflicting achievements in the final unity.

Some hint of Whitehead's position can be found in his conception of God as necessarily good. In one place he writes:

> The revolts of destructive evil, purely self-regarding, are dismissed into their triviality of mere individual facts; and yet the good they did achieve in individual joy, in individual sorrow, in the introduction of needed contrast, is yet saved by its relation to the completed whole.[25]

Once the world is prehended by God's consequent nature, there is no obstruction. But in the integration with his primordial side, there must be an attenuated importance of the "revolts of destructive evil"; and here, parenthetically, we may find another point that accords with Bradley. God salvages from the wreckage. The truth of the individual facts remain, but the good achieved reaches a higher harmonization in God's nature. He is the fellow sufferer with the world, prehending every actuality just as it is. But God uses the goodness achieved for his own vision of what the world may become in some unrealized future.

Clearly Whitehead's position is not wholly compatible with Bradley. There are elements of the Galilean vision of God as love, or God the poet central to Whitehead's conception, and this would not at all accurately characterize Bradley's entirely secularized

Absolute. But in another respect, the notion that goodness and beauty reach a higher harmonization with God's wisdom does square with Bradley's notion that such appearances involve less transformation in the final unity and therefore conduce to a higher Reality. This is not to say that, for Whitehead, goodness is more real; it is simply valued more by God in his function as Prime Mover. Evil and ugliness are never eliminated from the world. They are, in fact, required for various forms of contrast that save the world from bland monotony. God's vision, then, does include his desire for contrast, but the fact that each occasion only approximates the ideal set by God means that failures and various forms of destructive evil are inevitable.

Obviously one crucial point of divergence in Whitehead's position concerns the openness of the future for God. Since, for Whitehead, both God and the world are in the grip of the ultimate metaphysical ground of process, neither reaches a final completion or perfection. In order to understand exactly where Whitehead parts company with Bradley here, let us return to the essential doctrine of mutual immanence or harmony of opposites.

Although for Bradley all finite appearances belong together in one all-embracing Experience, it is just as true for him that the one Absolute is present in each of its many parts. So not only is it true for him that appearance is reality; it is equally true that reality is appearance. The many are One, and the One is many.

It is indeed tempting to see this same dialectical relationship repeated in Whitehead's philosophy when, in his analysis of ideal opposites, he concludes that none of the concepts—God, permanence, eternity, unity, or the One—can be understood without reference to their opposites—the world, flux, actuality, diversity, or the many.[26] But a more careful examination reveals that, whereas for Bradley, these opposites are interpreted in terms of one final timeless order, for Whitehead, the universe continually weaves itself between the opposites such that new orders evolve with the creative advance into novelty. The key concept, for Whitehead, is that universal relativity (mutual immanence) does not stop with the consequent nature of God. If it did, his God would not be altogether different from Bradley's Absolute. Instead, Whitehead's God is open at one end since the future is indeterminate. It should also be clear that God is not the *only* real Individual, as is commonly held in monistic philosophies (e.g. Spinoza's God/Nature, Bradley's Absolute), but one divine and eternal actual entity that moves *with* the whole of creation. He is only absolute as regards the absorption of the past. In the immediate present, however, there remains the multiplicity of contemporary actual occasions moving through their concrescence, and this multitude will only become one with God once they have individually reached their satisfaction. Whitehead's position, therefore, remains pluralistic.

As we saw above, God embodies both permanence and flux in his twofold nature. But since God can only prehend what has already become determinate in the immediate past, the present and the future are genuinely open for him as well. In fact, the whole concept of freedom requires that God cannot be omnipotent. God is therefore open in the sense that he is never complete. But whatever is decided in the temporal world, God is always there in a unison of immediacy to receive the outcome.

This very concept constitutes Whitehead's most radical divergence from both Western philosophic thought and orthodox theology: God too is in process. In his criticism of previous systems, Whitehead argues: "The vicious separation of the flux from the permanence leads to the concept of an entirely static God, with eminent reality, in relation to an entirely fluent world, with deficient reality."[27] But if the flux essentially qualifies God, the divine life too acquires a new life and refreshment with each successive stage of the universe, and in turn, he provides the ideal for the novel order in the present. "What is done in the world is transformed into a reality in heaven, and the reality in heaven passes back into the world."[28]

The idea that God is dynamic, creating and flowing with the world, yet saving it by absorbing every detail of finite achievement has certain advantages over the traditional Judeo-Christian conception. It has been the central idea that has inspired a whole school of process theology. But there are difficulties in Whitehead's conception of God as one actual entity, at least insofar as we take seriously his claim that God is the chief exemplification of the metaphysical principles. Indeed, in most cases, the problems that arise with Whitehead's God are a result of inconsistencies with the rest of the metaphysical principles.

Despite the analogies with actual occasions, it is far from clear how this conception of God as chief exemplification can be maintained.[29] Even though God, like ordinary actual occasions, is dipolar, essentially a mass of 'feeling' and a diversity in unity, God cannot accomplish what the occasions of the temporal world can, namely, satisfaction, or completion of the process of becoming.

It seems clear enough that Whitehead thought of God as an exception here especially since satisfaction requires perishing. God must therefore be regarded as a creative advance devoid of perishing. He is always becoming, even though as primordial keeper of the eternal objects, he is also eternal being. God therefore differs from ordinary actual occasions in the sense that he is an "everlasting concrescence" that reaches satisfaction only in the sense that, at each moment, he delights and suffers with the world as it passes into his consequent nature.

But the inability to reach satisfaction creates yet another difficulty. If God does not reach a completed stage of his concrescence (being), he cannot be objectified in order to provide initial aims for the occasions beginning a new concrescence. In other words, since God is always open, there is no determinate entity to function as 'object' for the actual occasions of the temporal world. This we shall call the "problem of causal independence." According to the metaphysical principles, two contemporary occasions of experience cannot prehend each other. But God, as an everlasting concrescence, is always subjectively immediate, and cannot, therefore, influence a present occasion in its novel becoming.

Modification of some sort is certainly required here, and Whiteheadians have for years sought various alternatives to Whitehead's view.[30] The main problem confronting Whitehead is how God is to be conceived as a temporal entity. This is indeed a very difficult problem.

One way out of the difficulty is to conceive of God's experience as happening in one grand epochal moment or specious present. Proceeding along these lines we would be approaching Bradley's or Royce's conception of the Absolute as that Individual whose time span overlaps all others, whose temporal epoch is such that within it, all other temporal epochs are encompassed.

This would solve the problem of causal independence because all the actual occasions—past, present, and future—would be subjectively immediate in God's experience, and there would be no need of initial aims. In effect, the order in the world would be aboriginal rather than continually evolving, and God's physical experience of the world would be analogous to his conceptual experience of the realm of eternal objects. But quite clearly, this would abandon the whole notion of God's creative advance *with* the world because God would be bound on both ends of time, and all would be determinate within. We would be left with one final order of permanent and static completion. Hartshorne, criticizing this view, remarks: "A God who eternally knew all that the fulfillment of his purpose would bring could have no need of that fulfillment or of purpose."[31]

But how else are we to conceive of God's experience as temporal? Hartshorne has attempted to solve the problem of causal independence by conceiving of God as a personally ordered 'society' of divine occasions.[32] On this modification of Whitehead's doctrine, God is a "stream of experience" analogous to that of human consciousness, and, at first sight, this idea does seem promising. Instead of being purely subjectively immediate, God's experience is subjective-becoming-objective (i.e., predecessors objectified in successors). According to this idea, God's antecedent states (as objectified) are capable of interaction with the world. However, aside from the obvious anthropomorphism, this modification generates new problems that do not necessarily apply to Whitehead. In particular, this view of God runs into the difficulty of reconciling a general creative advance with the denial by relativity physics of a cosmic simultaneity. Since God's experience happens as a succession of occasions, his prehension of the world would require a cosmic now. Each divine occasion would have to be almost instantaneous, yet fill all of space.[33] Moreover, on this view, Hartshorne seems to approach the idea of God's experience of the world as contained in a cosmic memory since his antecedent states accumulate in the present occasion. But here we would have to distinguish between the real event as it was in the temporal world and the memory of it in God's mind.[34]

Perhaps Whitehead recognized some of the difficulties in this conception when he chose to view God as *one* actual entity as opposed to an actual occasion. He wished to emphasize the permanent, eternal character of God that absorbs every detail of the world in everlasting harmony; while at the same time he wished to emphasize the idea that God sets the ideal for what the world can achieve. On the former view, his affinity to Bradley is quite clear. Whitehead saw in Bradley's Absolute a model for the One that preserves the many without loss or fading. But on the latter view, Whitehead's qualification that this One continually evolves *with* the world and therefore never reaches a static completion results in his inability to account for God's initial action on the world.

Much of this, I think, depends upon how we interpret God's incompleteness. As we have seen, the essential problem is that if God is genuinely open and never reaches satisfaction, then there cannot be an object to act on the present. But at one point, Whitehead does mention the superjective nature of God as the "pragmatic value of his specific satisfaction qualifying the transcendent creativity in the various temporal instances."[35] And this idea appears again when he discusses the four phases in which the universe accomplishes its actuality.[36] Here he seems to imply that the movement of the universe from many to One, and One to many, does provide an internal satisfaction or objectification in God's experience.

What I think Whitehead means when he says that God does not reach a static completion is that there is always room for novelty. There is always room for some unrealized achievement to become part of God's nature. But as each moment completes itself and passes into his consequent nature, there is an internal or momentary satisfaction in God. As one divine entity, God continually absorbs the data of the temporal world to formulate his own ideal vision, which in turn, acts back onto the world.

But how does this solve the problem of causal independence? On this view we have a process within a process: the latter is God as an everlasting concrescence, never complete and always moving with the world; while the former is that of internal satisfaction—God as enriched by the world as each occasion passes into his aesthetic harmony. Even though the many continually add to the One (i.e., the weaving of the physical into the conceptual), the One is always there for each new occasion to receive its ideal.

For each occasion, God is complete at the instant of its becoming. There is, at that time, the vision that God has for the world. But for God, the world is incomplete since there is no sense in which actual occasions come to an end.

Whitehead's admirable precision and accuracy of detail seem to fail him when he attempts to reconcile his conception of God with the mechanics of his cosmology. It is as if his romantic mode of expression and his classic, rational mode of expression clash once he attempts to integrate the two in his natural theology. But if the details of Whitehead's description of God are lacking, it is not altogether different from Bradley's repeated claim that the details of the Absolute completely escape finite judgment. With both philosophers, we seem to be left with an understanding of reality in broad outline. But in the end, whether one sides with Bradley, that all moments *are* just eternally there in the Absolute experience, or with Whitehead, that all moments *become* elements in God's consequent nature, the result is indeed "not so greatly different." As we speculate on the succession of moments, we are inspired with a sense of the importance of our actions as we realize how each forms part of an eternity beyond.

Epilogue

In the previous chapters, I attempted to bring to focus points of contact between Whitehead and Bradley and show how the central doctrine of 'feeling' provides a common bond uniting their respective philosophies. It was here that we found general agreement as to how a metaphysics of experience attempts to replace the materialist or physicalist conception of the universe. But I have also attempted to expose the differences between Whitehead and Bradley beginning with the problem of relations. In this respect, I have argued Whitehead's position over Bradley's in an attempt to defend:

1. the pluralistic interpretation of the world in which science and metaphysics can be seen as developing concurrently as opposed to the radically monistic interpretation in which the aims of science and metaphysics are sharply distinguished;
2. the general notion of creative advance and evolving order in opposition to the idea of a final and perfect order;
3. the reality of process and time as opposed to the relative unreality of time;
4. the idea of a genuine freedom of choice and the openness of the future as opposed to the idea that the whole of time is determinately fixed within the experience of the Absolute.

But even though Whitehead's views on these points have been found to be more satisfactory than Bradley's, it is clear that there are difficulties in the process view that do not arise in Bradley's eternalistic view of the universe. This came to surface in our final chapter where inconsistencies were found in Whitehead's conception of God. But whether or not the solutions offered above proved satisfactory, these problems do not seem insurmountable.

Even though Bradley's system, in the end, might be seen as more internally consistent, the idea that the whole of history, past, present, and future is eternally present in the Absolute is just as perplexing as Whitehead's idea that the history of the universe accumulates in God's consequent nature.

To admit a certain ambivalence here does not overthrow the conclusions of this essay, for this is just one of the central questions of speculative philosophy that inspires more accurate solutions.

ABBREVIATIONS OF WHITEHEAD'S
MAJOR WORKS

AE   *The Aims of Education*, 1929.

AI   *Adventures of Ideas*, 1933.

CN   *The Concept of Nature*, 1920.

ESP   *Essays in Science and Philosophy*, 1947.

FR   *The Function of Reason*, 1929.

IM   *An Introduction to Mathematics*, 1911.

IS   *Interpretation of Science,* ed., A. H. Johnson, 1961.

MT   *Modes of Thought*, 1938.

OT   *The Organisation of Thought*, 1917.

PM   *Principia Mathematica* (with Bertrand Russell) Vols I–III.

PNK   *An Enquiry Concerning the Principles of Natural Knowledge*, 1919.

PR   *Process and Reality*, 1929.

PRel   *The Principle of Relativity*, 1922.

RM   *Religion in the Making*, 1926.

SYM   *Symbolism, Its Meaning and Effect*, 1927.

SMW   *Science and the Modern World*, 1925.

UA   *A Treatise on Universal Algebra*, 1898.

ABBREVIATIONS OF BRADLEY'S
MAJOR WORKS

AR   *Appearance and Reality,* 1893.
CE   *Collected Essays,* Vols. I and II, 1935.
ES   *Ethical Studies,* 1876.
ETR   *Essays on Truth and Reality,* 1914.
PL   *Principles of Logic,* Vols. I and II, 1883.

NOTES

1. INTRODUCTION

1. *FR*, pp. 18–24, 39–42, and *AI*, chap. VII.

2. *ESP*, p. 88.

3. *PR*, p. xiii.

4. Ibid.

5. *ESP*, p. 88.

6. *AR*, p. 511.

7. Hicks, *Critical Realism*, p. 22. Also see my contribution to Lowe, *Whitehead: Man and Work*, Vol. 2, chaps. V and VI.

8. *IS*, pp. 155–56.

9. *CN*, p. 4

10. *CN*, p. 2

11. *CN*, p. 3.

12. *PNK*, p. vii.

13. *PR*, p. xii.

14. Lowe, *Whitehead: Man and Work*, Vol. 2, p. 333.

15. *AI*, p. 154.

16. *RM*, p. 84.

17. *FR*, p. 76.

18. *PR*, p. 189.

19. *RM*, p. 76.

20. *PR*, p. 42.

21. *PR*, p. 4.

22. *PR*, p. 8.

23. Whitehead has been compared to Alexander on this criticism. See, for example, Passmore, *Hundred Years of Philosophy*, p. 340. Also see Whittemore, "Whitehead's Process and Bradley's Reality," pp. 61–62.

24. On this point there is even a strong indication that the complete categoreal scheme was one of the last stages of Whitehead's composition of *Process and Reality*. See Ford, *Emergence of Whitehead's Metaphysics*, chap. 9, sec. J; and p. 192.

25. *PL*, Vol. 1, p. x.

26. Taylor, *Proceedings of the British Academy*, Vol. 21, p. 458. Cf. Muirhead, *Contemporary British Philosophy*, p. 11.

27. *PL*, Vol. 1, p. 151.

28. *PL*, Vol. 2, p. 515; *AR*, p. 508n.

29. *AR*, p. vii. This turns out to be a very strict sense of the term, for clearly Bradley's logic and metaphysics provide a system or scheme of first principles. The denial that his philosophy is a system must be understood in light of his conviction that finite intelligence cannot give a detailed account of the Absolute's structure.

30. *AR*, p. 1

31. *ETR*, p. 3.

32. *AR*, p. 120.

33. *PL*, Vol. 1, pp. 146–47.

34. *AR*, p. 130.

35. This necessity distinguishes his Absolute from that of Hegel, in which contradiction essentially qualifies Reality.

36. *PL*, Vol. 2, p. 431.

37. Wollheim, *F. H. Bradley*, pp. 17–18.

38. *PL*, Vol. 1, p. 117.

39. *ETR*, pp. 17–18.

40. James, *Radical Empiricism*, p. 98ff, and *Pluralistic Universe*, p. 43ff.

41. *AR*, p. 29.

42. Wollheim, *F. H. Bradley*, pp. 90–91.

43. Although the term *naturalized metaphysics* is more or less borrowed from W. V. Quine, I am using it in a different sense to characterize Whitehead's view of metaphysics as continuous with cosmology and science. See *Ontological Relativity*, p. 26, and *Logical Point of View*, pp. 44–45.

44. *CE*, Vol. 2, pp. 364–86.

45. *AR*, pp. 250–51.

46. Cf. discussion in chap. 5, pp. 111–123 of this work.

47. *AR*, p. x.

2. THE METAPHYSICS OF EXPERIENCE

1. *ETR*, pp. 444–45. Also see James Bradley, "Critique of Pure Feeling", p. 253.

2. *PR*, p. 189.

3. Leibniz, *Monadology*, sec. 14, p. 224.

4. Royce, *World and Individual*, Vol. 2, p. 240.

5. Ibid., p. 228.

6. James, *Principles of Psychology*, Vol. 1, pp. 148–49. (Emphasis his.)

7. *SMW*, p. 102.

8. Cf. Waddington, *Theoretical Biology*, Vol. 1, pp. 1–32; Vol. 2, pp. 72–81.

9. Sprigge, "Metaphysical Enquiry," p. 140. Also see his *Vindication of Absolute Idealism*, chaps. 1 and 3.

10. *PL*, Vol. 1, p. 95.

11. *AR*, pp. 332–33.

12. *ETR*, p. 194.

13. *ETR*, p. 189.

14. *ETR*, p. 173.

15. *ETR*, p. 194.

16. *ETR*, p. 174.

17. *AR*, p. 465.

18. *ETR*, p. 420.

19. *ETR*, p. 412.

20. Though employed in a slightly different sense, these terms are borrowed from Sprigge's *Vindication of Absolute Idealism*. See especially pp. 10–38.

21. *CE*, Vol. 2, p. 688.

22. *ETR*, p. 421.

23. A discrepancy immediately arises if the term *enduring* is chosen to describe the centres. We must therefore distinguish point of view. That is, if we view the centres from the side of the Absolute, they are better described as eternal and timeless. But from our perspective, this timeless character of the centre appears as endurance. That is, its self-identical character throughout momentary qualifications makes it enduring to us. I choose to adopt the term *enduring* rather than *eternal* because our primary concern is immediate experience from the point of view of human consciousness. See *AR*, p. 199.

24. Eliot, "Leibniz's Monads and Bradley's Finite Centres," reprinted as App. II of *Knowledge and Experience*, p. 200. This book was originally Eliot's Ph.D. dissertation submitted to the philosophy faculty of Harvard University.

25. *ETR*, pp. 414–15.

26. *ETR*, p. 410.

27. *ETR*, p. 424.

28. *ETR*, p. 169. Also see p. 173.

29. *ETR*, p. 410.

30. *AR*, p. 198.

31. *AR*, p. 407.

32. *AR*, p. 223.

33. Cf. *ETR*, p. 157, and *CE*, Vol. 2, p. 696.

34. *AR*, p. 215.

35. *AR*, p. 494.

36. *AR*, p. 127.

37. *AR*, p. 231.

38. *AR*, p. 239.

39. *AR*, p. 240.

40. Cf. *ETR*, pp. 350–51, and *AR*, p. 304.

41. *AR*, p. 241.

42. *AR*, p. 466. Also see *ETR*, pp. 350–51.

43. *AR*, p. 467.

44. Though Whitehead sometimes uses *actual entity* and *actual occasion* interchangeably, he does make a distinction in that the use of *actual occasion* excludes God from its scope. I shall consistently employ the term *actual occasion* in this essay to emphasize the event character of process. *Actual entity* will be reserved for God only. See, for example, *PR*, p. 87.

45. *PR*, p. 19.

46. See Sprigge, "Distinctiveness of American Philosophy", in Caws, ed., *Two Centuries of Philosophy in America*, p. 202.

47. *AI*, p. 221.

48. *PR*, p. 162. "Consciousness only illuminates the more primitive types of prehension so far as these prehensions are still elements in the products of integration. Thus those elements of our experience which stand out clearly and distinctly in our consciousness are not its basic facts; they are the derivative modifications which arise in the process." Also cf. *PR*, p. 236 and Bradley's *ETR*, p. 194.

49. *PR*, p. 176.

50. *PR*, pp. 176–77.

51. Russell, *Portraits from Memory*, p. 40f.

52. "The reason that I call my doctrine logical atomism is because the atoms that I wish to arrive at as the sort of last residue in analysis are logical atoms and not physical atoms. Some of them will be what I

call "particulars"—such things as little patches of colour or sounds, momentary things—and some of them will be predicates or relations and so on." Russell, *Logic and Knowledge*, pp. 178–9.

53. Cf. *PR*, p. 137; *MT*, p. 90.

54. Cf. *PR*, p. 11, and Price, *Dialogues of Whitehead*, p. 14.

55. *MT*, p. 121.

56. *PR*, p. 200.

57. *AI*, p. 231. Also see chap. 3, pp. 68–72 of this work.

58. *PR*, p. 80

59. *PR*, p. 21.

60. We must not be misled that this activity of creative choosing has moved us to a level of complex human consciousness. Such a feature is generic to all actual occasions throughout the universe. In short, we are still focusing primarily within the primitive level of causal efficacy which involves degrees of conscious selection but not of consciousness.

61. *PR*, p. xiii.

3. THE ANALYSIS OF EXPERIENCE

1. *PR*, p. 4.

2. *CE*, Vol. 2, p. 662.

3. *ESP*, p. 15.

4. *PR*, pp. 220–21, 235.

5. *AI*, p. 221; *PR*, p. 4.

6. *PR*, p. 162.

7. James, *Principles of Psychology*, Vol. 1, p. 605.

8. Ibid., p. 631. (Emphasis his.)

9. Ibid., p. 608.

10. Ibid., pp. 609–10.

11. James, *Radical Empiricism*, p. 95.

12. *ETR*, p. 157n.

13. *ETR*, p. 412.

14. *PL*, Vol. 1, p. 52.

15. Ibid., pp. 54–56. Also cf. *AR*, pp. 223–24.

16. Ibid., p. 56.

17. Ibid., p. 53.

18. Later, in *SMW*, Whitehead called this view the "fallacy of simple location," the notion that bits of matter can be simply located here in time or here in space, and held up on either side by purely external supports.

19. *PNK*, p. 8; *CN*, pp. 57, 68.

20. *CN*, p. 56.

21. *CN*, p. 189.

22. The idea of narrowing perceptible durations is illustrated by the notions of "whole-part" relations and "overlapping" in which events extend over one another in a pattern like a nest of Chinese boxes. The point, of course, lies at the center but is only reached as a logical end of the narrowing process. *PNK*, p. 105; *CN*, chap. IV. Also see my chapter VI in Lowe, *Whitehead: Man and Work*, Vol. 2, especially pp. 114–23.

23. See, for example, *CN*, pp. 56, 59, 69.

24. *CN*, p. 69.

25. *PNK*, p. vii.

26. *CN*, p. 5.

27. *PNK*, p. 202.

28. One admirable attempt to work out the development of these ideas has been undertaken by Lewis Ford. See especially chap. 2 and 3 of *Emergence of Whitehead's Metaphysics*.

29. *PR*, p. 68.

30. For an examination of Zeno's four paradoxes of motion, see Robinson, *Early Greek Philosophy*, pp. 131–36.

31. *PR*, p. 68.

32. *PR*, p. 35. Also cf. *SMW*, p. 126.

33. *IS*, p. 246.

34. *PR*, p. 69.

35. *PR*, p. 283.

36. *ETR*, p. 173.

37. *PL*, Vol. 1, p. 101.

38. Ibid.

39. *AR*, p. 555.

40. *PR*, p. 154.

41. *PR*, p. 211.

42. *PR*, p. 29.

43. For a more detailed exposition of the phases of the concrescence, see Donald Sherburne's splendid work, *A Key to Whitehead's Process and Reality*, chap. 3.

44. *PR*, p. 50.

45. Here I follow Sherburne in distinguishing these two final stages. *A Key to Whitehead's Process and Reality*, p. 39.

46. See Lowe, *Understanding Whitehead*, p. 43n.

47. The notion of horizontal or vertical dimensions of an actual occasion is, of course, entirely for illustration.

48. *PR*, p. 239.

49. *PR*, p. 248.

50. *PR*, p. 279.

51. *PR*, p. 280.

52. *PR*, p. 280.

53. *PR*, p. 266.

54. *PR*, p. 267.

55. *PR*, p. 267.

56. *ETR*, pp. 192–98.

57. *PR*, p. 215.

58. *AI*, p. 231, from *ETR*, p. 159.

59. *ETR*, p. 171 (misquoted as p. 161.)

60. *AI*, pp. 231–32.

61. *AI*, p. 233.

62. *ETR*, p. 181.

63. *ETR*, p. 166n.

64. *ETR*, p. 171.

65. *ETR*, p. 168.

66. *ETR*, p. 168.

67. *AI*, p. 232.

68. *ETR*, p. 182.

69. *ETR*, p. 188.

4. INTERNAL AND EXTERNAL RELATIONS

1. *AR*, chap. III.

2. Wollheim, *F. H. Bradley*, p. 109.

3. *AR*, p. 24.

4. *AR*, p. 26.

5. *AR*, p. 26.

6. *AR*, p. 27.

7. *AR*, p. 28.

8. *ETR*, p. 190.

9. Sprigge, "Bradley and Russell on Relations," in Roberts, ed., *Russell Memorial Volume*, p. 161. See also *AR*, pp. 522–24.

10. *PL*, Vol. 1, p. 96.

11. *AR*, p. 512: "They are not given except as contained in and as qualifying some whole, and their independence consists merely in our vicious abstraction. Nor when we pass to the relational stage does diversity cease to be the inseparable adjective of unity. For the relations

themselves cannot exist except within and as the adjectives of an underlying unity. The whole that is analysed into relations and terms can fall
into the background and be obscured, but it can never be dissipated."

12. *ETR*, p. 190.

13. For example, Hume writes: "Again, every thing, which is different, is distinguishable, and every thing which is distinguishable, is separable by the imagination. . . . My conclusion . . . is, that since all our
perceptions are different from each other, and from every thing else in
the universe, they are also distinct and separable, and may be consider'd
as separately existent, and may exist separately, and have no need of
anything else to support their existence." *Treatise of Human Nature*,
ed., Selby-Bigge, bk. 1, p. 4, sec. 5, p. 233.

14. *CN*, pp. 141–42.

15. James, *Pluralistic Universe*, p. 79.

16. Ibid., p. 73.

17. James, *Radical Empiricism*, pp. 47–49.

18. Ibid., p. 107.

19. Ibid., p. 62.

20. James, *Pluralistic Universe*, pp. 279–80.

21. Cf. *CE*, Vol. 2, pp. 654–55, and *ETR*, p. 149f.

22. James, *Some Problems of Philosophy*, pp. 92–93.

23. James, *Principles of Psychology*, Vol. 1, p. 241.

24. Cf. James *Pluralistic Universe*, pp. 69–70, 257–58. Also see
Radical Empiricism, pp. 50–51.

25. Cf. McTaggart, *Nature of Existence*, chaps. VIII and IX, and
Russell, *Principles of Mathematics*, pp. 99–100.

26. Russell, *Outline of Philosophy*, p. 263.

27. Lowe, *The Journal of Philosophy* 38 (1941); reprinted in *Understanding Whitehead*, p. 344. (Lowe's emphasis)

28. *AI*, p. 230. Also see his discussion of relations and contrasts,
PR, pp. 228–29.

29. For example, see *ETR*, pp. 176–77.

30. *PL*, Vol. 1, p. 96.

31. *CE*, Vol. 2, pp. 657–58.

32. On this score, even if Bradley's argument (2) is construed as addressing this very possibility, we still have the problem of his understanding of the relation as a substantial entity and no indication of any other way of understanding what the relation could be.

33. See Johnson, "On Prehending the Past," p. 263.

34. *PR*, p. 237.

35. *PL*, Vol. 1, p. 101.

36. *AR*, p. 464.

37. *PR*, p. 200.

38. *PR*, p. 50.

39. Russell, "On the Nature of Truth." Also see *My Philosophical Development*, pp. 54–64.

40. Russell, *Principles of Mathematics*, p. 221.

41. Ibid., p. 225.

42. For an example of the way in which asymmetrical relations may be seen as compatible with a Bradleian monism, see Sprigge, *Vindication of Absolute Idealism*, p. 241.

43. *CE*, Vol. 2, p. 671.

44. Of course in the strictest sense, Bradley cannot be taken to espouse a doctrine of internal relations, but for the purpose at hand this formulation will suffice.

45. *ETR*, p. 237.

46. Failure to understand this point has led some writers to suggest that pluralism and the doctrine of internal relations are incompatible in Whitehead. See especially Alston, "Internal Relatedness and Pluralism in Whitehead," pp. 535–58.

47. Cf. Hartshorne, *Creative Synthesis,* chap. X; *AI*, chap. XII.

48. *AI*, p. 195.

49. *AI*, p. 195. Even here Hartshorne insists that the relationship is still asymmetrical. The spatial relations of the contemporary nexus can only be related by causation or inheritance. See *Creative Synthesis*, p. 219. Spatial relations are "multiple lines of inheritance" and cannot interpenetrate.

50. Cf. *Creative Synthesis*, p. 211f, and *Reality as Social Process*, p. 70f.

51. The principle that *B* is dependent on *A*, but *A* is independent of *B* is never considered as an alternative.

52. *PR*, p. 327.

53. *PR*, p. 286.

54. *PR*, p. 309.

55. *PR*, p. 66.

56. *PR*, p. 66.

57. *PR*, p. 308.

58. *SMW*, p. 160. Although Whitehead had not developed the idea of prehending eternal objects at the time of *SMW*, it is clear that the asymmetry of this relationship between eternal objects and actual occasions holds throughout *PR* as well.

59. *SMW*, p. 171. Also see pp. 162–63.

60. *SMW*, p. 161.

61. *SMW*, p. 160.

62. *SMW*, p. 165.

63. Cf. Ford, *Emergence of Whitehead's Metaphysics*, pp. 78–86, to which I owe my understanding of these asymmetries.

64. *SMW*, p. 163. Also cf. *PRel*, pp. 18–19, for a similar analysis.

65. *SMW*, p. 169. Unlike the analysis of eternal objects in pure abstraction, when Whitehead's concern is with the "real togetherness" of eternal objects as components of actual occasions, he makes a crucial distinction between "contrasts" and relations. Contrasts are *particulars* with individual definiteness, like the contrast between red and blue perceived in a moment of perception. They are particular modes of synthesis where difference is held in unity. A relation, on the other hand, is found among many different types of contrasts, but in this sense, the relation is a mere abstraction from the various types of concrete relatedness. A relation is therefore a genus of contrasts, and as Bradley discovered, it fails to do the job of contrasts. The abstract universal characterizes many different types of relatedness, but as a spearate entity in a relational situation, it fails to do the real work of connecting. See *PR*, pp. 228–29.

66. Others have found Bradley's point to be entirely unintelligible. Brand Blanshard, for example, argues that Bradley's distinction itself is a distinction without difference. See "Bradley on Relations" in Manser and Stock, eds., *Philosophy of Bradley*, pp. 216–17.

67. *ESP*, p. 81.

68. Emmet, *Whitehead's Philosophy of Organism*, p. 57.

5. EXTENSION AND WHOLE-PART RELATIONS

1. *PR*, p. 163.

2. *AR*, p. 236.

3. Strawson, *Individuals*, p. 38.

4. Ibid., p. 55.

5. Ibid., pp. 59–60.

6. *PR*, p. 73.

7. Strawson, *Individuals*, p. 181ff.

8. *PR*, p. 11.

9. Davidson, "The Individuation of Events," in *Essays on Actions and Events*, pp. 163–80. For a more recent analysis of events in the tradition of descriptive, or conservative, metaphysics, see Bennett, *Events and Their Names*.

10. Davidson, *Essays on Actions and Events*, p. 174.

11. It might be objected that Strawson does consider unit-events as centers of consciousness in his criticism of a version of Leibniz's monadism. The point, as in the purely auditory world, is that the essential conditions of reference could not be satisfied with particulars that were not of a spatio-temporal character. But I think here, as in the case of sounds, the real events cannot be deprived of their extensive characteristics. They necessarily involve a lapse of time as well as an extension in space, and in the end, it is not clear whether Strawson's version of Leibniz's monadism does justice to the intricate system of perceptions in which space and time arise out of the relations between monads.

12. Hartshorne, *Creative Synthesis*, pp. 173–74.

13. Dobzhansky, *Genetics and Evolutionary Process*, p. 22.

14. *AI*, p. 185.

15. Jones, et al., *Atoms and the Universe*, p. 138.

16. Folse, "Complementarity," p. 261.

17. *PR*, p. 40, 46.

18. *PR*, p. 177.

19. *MT*, p. 188.

20. *MT*, p. 192.

21. *SMW*, p. 136.

22. *AI*, p. 186.

23. See chapter 2, p. 27 of this work.

24. *MT*, p. 205.

25. *AR*, p. 162.

26. *ETR*, p. 412.

27. *AR*, p. 214.

28. Royce, *World and Individual*, Vol. 1, p. 261. Also see Sprigge, *Vindication of Absolute Idealism*, chap. IV.

29. *AI*, p. 204.

30. *PR*, p. 112.

31. *MT*, p. 210.

32. *PR*, p. 34.

33. *AI*, p. 204.

34. *PR*, p. 92.

35. *PR*, p. 103.

36. *PR*, p. 100.

37. *PR*, p. 102.

38. *PR*, p. 101.

39. Some doubt may be expressed here as to this purely temporal character since Whitehead always held to the ideal that all occasions carry extensive characteristics. My present occasion has a locus in space, namely, my present location. On this point, see Wolf, "Psychological Physiology," pp. 274–91.

40. For example, see Armstrong, *Materialist Theory of Mind.*

41. *SMW,* p. 107.

42. *SMW,* pp. 111–12.

43. C. H. Waddington, having developed some of these points along Whiteheadian lines, writes: "What we find is a whole complex cell becoming either a nerve or kidney or a muscle cell . . . the process of becoming (say) a nerve cell should be regarded as the result of the activities of large numbers of genes, which interact together to form a unified 'concrescence'." *Towards a Theoretical Biology,* Vol. 2, p. 80. And more generally: "the environment which exerts selection on one organism is influenced by the presence of other organisms; and as the other organisms change in evolution, so the environment of the first organism is altered, and it must evolve too." Ibid., p. 116.

44. *AR,* p. 442.

45. Cf. *CE,* Vol. 2, p. 596, and *AR,* pp. 186–91.

46. *PR,* p. 91.

47. Ibid.

48. *PR,* p. 97.

49. *PR,* p. 90.

50. *PR,* p. 66.

51. *PR,* p. 97.

52. *PR,* p. 92.

53. *PR,* pp. 288–89.

54. Chap. 4, pp. 93–96.

55. *PR,* p. 288.

56. *PR,* p. 289.

57. *MT,* pp. 211–12.

58. *PR,* p. 198.

59. *ESP,* p. 88; *PR,* pp. 43, 54, 156, 190, 200, 229.

60. *PR,* p. 111.

61. *PR,* p. 200.

62. *PR,* p. xiii.

63. Hocking, "Whitehead on Mind and Nature," in Schilpp, ed., *Philosophy of Alfred North Whitehead*, p. 386.

6. TIME

1. *AR*, p. 183.

2. Chap. 3, pp 50–53, and chap. 4, pp. 74–78.

3. *AR*, p. 186.

4. *AR*, p. 187.

5. *CE*, Vol. 1, "Why Do We Remember Forwards And Not Backwards?" p. 240–41.

6. *AR*, p. 189n.

7. *AR*, p. 190.

8. Fitzgerald, "The Curious Case of Benjamin Button," in *Tales of the Jazz Age*. The only inconsistency in this story is that Fitzgerald conceived of Benjamin's stream of consciousness as running forward instead of backward with the physical regression. Also, Benjamin's predicament is not a typical life in some possible world but rather an anomaly in his own.

9. For example, one may remember a past holiday abroad and trace the events from departure to returning home and on up to the present day.

10. *CE*, Vol. 1, p. 241.

11. Provided that Bradley wrote this paper on psychology in order to simply explain a mental phenomenon, it does not and was not intended to express his ultimate metaphysical position. However, I do think that it is consistent with his final conclusion that direction, temporal unity and memory are all ideal constructions from the present that serve our practical purposes and should not be taken as the final truth about the nature of reality.

12. Whitehead himself takes up this problem in his Presidential Address to the Aristotelian Society in 1922, "Uniformity and Contingency." Although his view at this time emphasized the primacy of extension over process, it is still clear that he saw the dominance of one space-time framework. He argues, for example:

> The distinction between the dream-world and nature is, that the space-time of the dream-world cannot conjoin with the scheme of the space-

time of nature, as constituted by any part of nature. The dream-world is no where at no time, though it has a dream-time and dream-space of its own . . .

The position we are led to is that we are aware of a dominant space-time continuum and that reality consists of the sense-objects projected into that continuum. It is not true that the apprehended process invariably fits into the dominant continuum: for example, dreams do not. But it is true that by direct inference we can always correlate the process of apprehension with the dominant continuum: for example, in the case of a dream we can note the time of going to bed and the time of waking, and can correlate the process of apprehending the dream with some portion of the intervening night. *ESP*, pp. 102–03.

13. *AR*, p. 187.

14. *AI*, p. 191.

15. Plato, *Timaeus*, in Cornford, *Plato's Cosmology*, p. 98.

16. Santayana, *Realm of Matter*, pp. 86–91.

17. In large measure I derive my understanding of the compatibility of the eternalistic theory of time and the doctrine of the Absolute from T. L. S. Sprigge. See especially, *Vindication of Absolute Idealism*, pp. 30–33, and chap. 6. Also, for detailed discussion of Santayana's theory of time, see Sprigge, *Santayana*, chap. IX, and "Ideal Immortality."

18. *PL*, Vol. 1, p. 70.

19. *ETR*, p. 426.

20. Cf. chap. 2, p. 32 of this work.

21. *ETR*, p. 410.

22. *ETR*, p. 424.

23. *ETR*, p. 427. (My emphasis.)

24. Santayana, *Realm of Truth*, pp. 79–80.

25. Also on this comparison, see Sprigge, *Santayana*, p. 231, n. 12.

26. Santayana, *Realm of Truth*, p. 82.

27. Ibid., p. 85.

28. Ibid., p. 83.

29. *PR*, pp. 12–13.

30. *PR*, pp. 209, 338. Poem by Henry Francis Lyte in hymn by William Henry Monk.

31. Sprigge, *Vindication of Absolute Idealism*, pp. 225–32. Also see n. 17 above.

32. Sprigge, "Ideal Immortality," p. 230.

33. Sprigge, *Vindication of Absolute Idealism*, p. 230.

34. Ibid., p. 231.

35. Actually Sprigge here uses the pharse "imaginative sympathy," but I think the main point of grasping the reality of another as a state of consciousness is the same. For instance, he writes: "to grasp something of the very essence of a reality by actualizing it in one's own mind and attributing it to that reality beyond seems to me knowledge of the deepest and most concrete sort." Ibid., p. 5.

36. Letter from Whitehead to Dorothy Emmet. See Emmet, *Whitehead's Philosophy of Organism*, p. xxiv.

37. *PR*, p. 340.

38. Ibid.

39. *PR*, p. 13.

40. *PR*, p. 12.

41. Sprigge, "Ideal Immortality," p. 227.

42. *PR*, p. 338.

43. *PR*, p. 346.

44. *PR*, p. 13.

45. *PR*, p. 259.

46. Here we note the difference between judgments and propositions. Whitehead held that propositions are "entertained" as lures for 'feeling,' whereas judgments are true or false because they arise out of integrations between the eternal objects as possibilities and actual facts. See Emmet, *Whitehead's Philosophy of Organism*, pp. 164–67.

47. Sprigge, *Vindication of Absolute Idealism*, p. 142.

7. GOD AND THE ABSOLUTE

1. *PR*, p. xiii.

2. *ESP*, p. 89.

3. *AR*, p. 458.

4. *AR*, p. 470, 140–41, 494.

5. *AR*, p. 215.

6. *AR*, pp. 426–27.

7. *AR*, p. 469. Also see pp. 371, 414.

8. Cf. *AR*, pp. 412, 371, 414, 469.

9. *AR*, p. 431.

10. *AR*, p. 180.

11. *AR*, p. 180.

12. *AR*, p. 453.

13. *ETR*, p. 348.

14. *ETR*, p. 469.

15. *ESP*, p. 90.

16. *PR*, p. 343.

17. *PR*, pp. 350–51.

18. *ETR*, p. 348.

19. *PR*, p. 346.

20. R. C. Whittemore has made this comparison quite clear in a paper entitled, "Whitehead's Process and Bradley's Reality," p. 71.

21. *PR*, p. 346.

22. *MT*, pp. 70–71.

23. *PR*, p. 345.

24. *PR*, p. 345.

25. *PR*, p. 346. Also see *RM*, p. 83.

26. See especially *PR*, p. 348.

27. *PR*, p. 346. Also see, *ESP*, p. 88, and *MT*, p. 109.

28. *PR*, p. 351.

29. See especially Whittemore, "Time and Whitehead's God."

30. See especially Ford, "Divine Activity of the Future," pp. 169–70. Also see *Two Process Philosophers*, pp. 36–37, 66–67.

31. Hartshorne, *Logic of Perfection*, p. 205.

32. Ibid., pp. 92–93; Hartshorne, *Creative Synthesis*, p. xv.

33. Ford, *Two Process Philosophers*, p. 36.

34. Sprigge, "Ideal Immortality," p. 227.

35. *PR*, p. 88.

36. *PR*, pp. 350–51.

BIBLIOGRAPHY

Alston, W. P. "Internal Relatedness and Pluralism in Whitehead." *Review of Metaphysics* 5 (1952).

Ariel, R. A. "A Mathematical Root of Whitehead's Cosmological Thought." *Process Studies* 4 (1974).

Armstrong, D. A. *A Materialist Theory of Mind*. London: Routledge & Kegan Paul, 1968.

Barnhart, J. E. "Bradley's Monism and Whitehead's Neo-Pluralism." *The Southern Journal of Philosophy* 7 (1969–70).

Bedell, Gary. "The Relation of Logic and Metaphysics in the Philosophy of F. H. Bradley." *The Modern Schoolman* 48 (1971).

Bennett, Jonathan. *Events and Their Names*. Indianapolis: Hackett Publishing Co., 1988.

Bergson, Henri. *Creative Evolution*. London: Macmillan and Co., 1911.

Bigger, Charles. "Objects and Events." *The Southern Journal of Philosophy* 11 (1973).

Bosanquet, Bernard. *The Principle of Individuality and Value*. London: Macmillan and Co., 1912.

Bradley, F. H. *Appearance and Reality*. Oxford: Oxford University Press, 1978.

———. *Collected Essays*. Vols. 1 and 2. Oxford: Oxford University Press, 1935.

———. *Essays on Truth and Reality*. Oxford: Oxford University Press, 1914.

———. *Principles of Logic*. Vols. 1 and 2. Oxford: Oxford University Press, 1922.

Bradley, James. "'The Critique of Pure Feeling': Bradley, Whitehead, and the Anglo-Saxon Metaphysical Tradition." *Process Studies* 14 (4) (1985).

Burtt, E. A. *The Metaphysical Foundations of Modern Science*. London: Kegan Paul, Treach, Trubner, and Co., 1925.

Casey, G. S. "Keeping the Past in Mind." *Review of Metaphysics* 37 (1983).

Caws, Peter, ed. *Two Centuries of Philosophy in America*. Totowa, NJ: Rowman & Littlefield, 1980.

Christian, William A. *An Interpretation of Whitehead's Metaphysics*. New Haven: Yale University Press, 1959.

Church, R. W. *Bradley's Dialectic*. London: Allen & Unwin,1942.

Cornford, Francis. *Plato's Cosmology*. Indianapolis: Bobbs-Merrill Co., 1937.

Crossley, D. J. "Holism, Individualism and Internal Relations." *Journal of the History of Philosophy* 15 (1977).

Cushin, W. E. *The Physical Cosmology of Alfred North Whitehead* Ph.D. thesis, Edinburgh University, 1951.

Datta, A. M. "Bradley's Conception of Degrees of Truth and Reality." *Pakistan Philosophical Journal* 3 (1966).

Davidson, Donald. *Essays on Actions and Events*. Oxford: Clarendon Press, 1980.

Dobzhansky, Theodosius. *Genetics of the Evolutionary Process*. New York: Columbia University Press, 1970.

Driesch, Hans. *The Science and Philosophy of Organism*. Aberdeen: Aberdeen University Press, 1908.

Eisendrath, C. R. *The Unifying Moment: The Psychological Philosophy of William James and Alfred North Whitehead*. Cambridge: Harvard University Press, 1971.

Eliot, T. S. *Knowledge and Experience in the Philosophy of F. H. Bradley*. London: Faber and Faber, 1964.

———. "Leibniz's Monads and Bradley's Finite Centres." *The Monist* 26 (1916).

Emmett, Dorothy. *The Effectiveness of Causes*. Albany: State University of New York Press, 1985.

———. "Language and Metaphysics: Introduction to a Symposium." *Theoria to Theory* 11 (1977).

————. *Whitehead's Philosophy of Organism.* Westport: Greenwood Press, 1966.

Ewing, A. C. *Idealism: A Critical Survey.* London: Methuen & Co., 1961.

Fitzgerald, F. Scott. *Tales of the Jazz Age.* New York: Scribners, 1922.

Folse, Henry. "Complementarity, Bell's Theorem, and the Framework of Process Metaphysics." *Process Studies* 11 (1981).

————. "The Copenhagen Interpretation of Quantum Theory and Whitehead's Philosophy of Organism." *Tulane Studies in Philosophy* 23 (1974).

Ford, Lewis S. "The Divine Activity of the Future." *Process Studies* 11 (1981).

————. *The Emergence of Whitehead's Metaphysics.* Albany: State University of New York Press, 1984.

————. ed. *Two Process Philosophers.* Tallahassee: American Academy of Religion, 1973.

Ford, Marcus Peter. *William James's Philosophy.* Amherst: University of Massachusetts Press, 1982.

Gale, R. M., ed. *The Philosophy of Time.* London: Macmillan and Co., 1968.

Gram, M. S. "The Reality of Relations." *New Scholasticism* 44 (1970).

Gross, M. W. "Whitehead's Answer to Hume." *Journal of Philosophy* 38 (1941).

Hall, Everett. "Of What Use Are Whitehead's Eternal Objects?" *Journal of Philosophy* 27 (1930).

Harrah, David. "The Influence of Logic and Mathematics on Whitehead." *Journal of Philosophy* 20 (1959).

Hartshorne, Charles. "The Case for Idealism." *Philosophical Forum* 1 (1968).

————. "Causal Necessities: An Alternative to Hume." *Review of Metaphysics* 63 (1954).

————. *Creative Synthesis and Philosophic Method.* London: SCM Press, 1970.

————. *The Logic of Perfection*. Lasalle: Open Court 1962.

————. "My Neoclassical Metaphysics." UIT *Tijdschrift Voor Filosofie* 42e, 1 (1980).

—————. "Neoclassical Metaphysics." *Philosophers on Their Own Work* 8 (1981).

————. *Reality as Social Process*. Glencoe, IL: The Free Press, 1953.

————. Review of *Genesis of Modern Process Thought: A Historical Outline with Bibliography*, by George R. Lucas, Jr. *Process Studies* 13 (1983).

Hicks, G. D. *Critical Realism*. London: Macmillan and Co., 1938.

Howie, J., and Buford, T. O., eds. *Contemporary Studies in Philosophical Idealism*. Cape Cod: Claude Stark and Co., 1975.

Huchingson, James. "Organization and Process: Systems Philosophy and Whiteheadian Metaphysics." *Process Studies* 11 (1981).

Hume, David. *A Treatise of Human Nature*. ed., L. A. Selby-Bigge. Oxford: Oxford University Press, 1978.

James, William. *Essays in Radical Empiricism*. New York: Longmans, Green and Co., 1912.

————. *A Pluralistic Universe*. New York: Longmans, Green and Co., 1909.

————. *Principles of Psychology*. Vols. 1 and 2. London: Macmillan and Co., 1891.

————. *Some Problems of Philosophy*. New York: Longmans, Green and Co., 1911.

Johnson, A. H. "Leibniz and Whitehead." *Philosophy and Phenomenological Research* 19 (1959).

Johnson, Charles M. "On Prehending the Past." *Process Studies* 6 (1976).

Jones, G. O., J. Rotblat, and G. J. Whitrow. *Atoms and the Universe*. Middlesex: Penguin, 1973.

Jordan, Martin. *New Shapes of Reality*. London: Allen & Unwin, 1968.

Kalupahana, David. "The Buddhist Conception of Time and Temporality." *Philosophy East and West* 24 (1974).

Kline, George L., ed. *Alfred North Whitehead: Essays on His Philosophy.* Englewood Cliffs: Prentice Hall, 1963.

Kneebone, G. T. *Mathematical Logic and the Foundations of Mathematics.* London: D. Van Nostrand Company, 1963.

Kulkarni, N. G. "Bradley's Anti-Relational Argument." *Philosophical Quarterly* 7 (1957).

Lango, John. *Whitehead's Ontology.* Albany: State University of New York Press, 1972.

Lawrence, Nathaniel. *Whitehead's Philosophical Development.* Berkeley: University of California Press, 1956.

Leclerc, Ivor. "Internal Relatedness in Whitehead: A Rejoinder." *Review of Metaphysics* 6 (1952–53).

———. ed. *The Relevance of Whitehead.* London: Allen & Unwin, 1961.

———. *Whitehead's Metaphysics.* Bloomington: Indiana University Press, 1975.

Leibniz, G. W., *Monadology.*, tr., Robert Latta. Oxford: Oxford University Press, 1965.

Lowe, Victor. *Alfred North Whitehead: The Man and His Work.* Baltimore: Johns Hopkins University Press, Vol. 1, 1985, Vol. 2, 1990.

———. *Understanding Whitehead.* Baltimore: Johns Hopkins University Press, 1966.

———. "William James and Whitehead's Doctrine of Prehensions." *The Journal of Philosophy* 38 (1941).

———. "Whitehead's Gifford Lectures." *The Southern Journal of Philosophy* 7 (1969–70).

Lucas, George R., Jr., ed. *Hegel and Whitehead.* Albany: State University of New York Press, 1986.

———. *The Rehabilitation of Whitehead.* Albany: State University of New York Press, 1990.

Mack, Robert D. *The Appeal to Immediate Experience: Philosophic Method in Bradley, Whitehead and Dewey.* New York: King's Crown Press, 1945.

Marcel, Gabriel. *Royce's Metaphysics*. Westport: Greenwood Press, 1975.

Manser, Anthony. *Bradley's Logic*. Totowa, NJ: Barnes & Noble Books, 1983.

Manser, Anthony, and Guy Stock, eds. *The Philosophy of F. H. Bradley*. Oxford: Oxford University Press, 1984.

Mays, Wolfe. *The Philosophy of Whitehead*. London: Allen & Unwin, 1959.

————. "Whitehead and the Philosophy of Time." *Studium Generale* 23 (1970).

McDougall, William. *Body and Mind*. London: Methuen and Co., 1911.

McHenry, Leemon. "Bradley, James and Whitehead on Relations." *The Journal of Speculative Philosophy* 3 (1989).

————. "The Axiomatic Matrix of Whitehead's *Process and Reality*." *Process Studies* 15 (1986).

————. "Time, Relations and Dependence." *The Southern Journal of Philosophy* 21 (1983).

McTaggart, J. M. E. *The Nature of Existence*. Cambridge: Cambridge University Press, Vol. 1, 1921, Vol. 2, 1927.

Muirhead, J. H. *Contemporary British Philosophy*. London: Allen and Unwin, 1924.

Nelson, A. F. "Internal Relations." *Southwestern Journal of Philosophy* 3 (1972).

O'Connor, D. J. O., ed. *A Critical History of Western Philosophy*. London: The Free Press, 1964.

Palter, Robert. *Whitehead's Philosophy of Science*. Chicago: University of Chicago Press, 1960.

Passmore, John. *A Hundred Years of Philosophy*. Middlesex: Pelican Books, 1968.

Pittenger, Norman. *Alfred North Whitehead*. London: Lutterworth Press, 1969.

Plamondon, A. L. *Whitehead's Organic Philosophy of Science*. Albany: State University of New York Press, 1979.

Plato. *Republic*. tr., Benjamin Jowett in *The Dialogues of Plato*. Vol. 2. Oxford: Oxford University Press, 1953.

Plato. *Timaeus*. tr., Benjamin Jowett in *The Dialogues of Plato*. Vol. 3. Oxford: Oxford University Press, 1953.

Polis, Edward. *Whitehead's Metaphysics*. Carbondale: Southern Illinois University Press, 1967.

Price, Lucien. *Dialogues of Alfred North Whitehead*. London: Max Reinhardt, 1954.

Quine, W. V. *From a Logical Point of View*. New York: Harper and Row, 1963.

———. *Ontological Relativity and Other Essays*. New York: Columbia University Press, 1969.

Rapp, Friedrich, and Reiner Wiehl, eds. *Whitehead's Metaphysics of Creativity*. Albany: State University of New York Press, 1990.

Roberts, George, ed. *Bertrand Russell Memorial Volume*. London: Allen & Unwin, 1979.

Robinson, J. M. *An Introduction to Early Greek Philosophy*. Boston: Houghton Mifflin Co., 1986.

Royce, Josiah. "Mind and Reality." *Mind* 7 (1882).

———. *The World and the Individual*. Vols 1 and 2. London: Macmillan and Company, 1901.

Russell, Bertrand. *Logic and Knowledge*. London: Allen & Unwin, 1956.

———. *My Philosophical Development*. London: Allen & Unwin, 1959.

———. "On the Nature of Truth." *Proceedings of the Aristotelian Society* (1906–7).

———. *Outline of Philosophy*. London: Allen & Unwin, 1961.

———. *Portraits From Memory*. London: Allen & Unwin, 1956.

———. *Principles of Mathematics*. London: Allen & Unwin, 1903.

Santayana, George. *The Realm of Essence*. London: Constable and Co., 1928.

———. *The Realm of Matter*. London: Constable and Co., 1930.

———. *The Realm of Truth*. London: Constable and Co., 1937.

———. *Skepticism and Animal Faith*. London: Constable and Co., 1923.

Saxena, S. K. *Studies in the Metaphysics of Bradley*. London: Allen & Unwin, 1967.

Schilpp, Paul, ed. *The Philosophy of Alfred North Whitehead* in the Library of Living Philosophers. New York: Tudor Publishing Co.,1941

Schmidt, Paul F. *Perception and Cosmology in Whitehead's Philosophy*. New Brunswick: Rutgers University Press, 1967.

Silkstone, T. W. "Bradley on Relations." *Idealistic Studies* 4 (1974).

Shahan, E. P. *Whitehead's Theory of Experience*. New York: Kings Crown Press, 1950.

Sherburne, Donald. *A Key to Whitehead's Process and Reality*. Bloomington: Indiana University Press, 1975.

Smart, J. J. C. "The Temporal Asymmetry of the World." *Analysis* 14 (1954).

Smith, Norman Kemp. *The Credibility of Divine Existence*, eds., A. J. D. Porteous, R. D. Maclennan, and G. E. Davie. London: Macmillan and Co., 1967.

___. *Prolegomena to an Idealist Theory of Knowledge*. London: Macmillan and Co., 1924.

Sprigge, T. L. S. "Ideal Immortality." *The Southern Journal of Philosophy* 10 (1972).

———. "The Importance of Subjectivity: An Inaugural Lecture." *Inquiry* 25 (1981).

———. "Knowledge of Subjectivity." *Theoria to Theory* 14 (1981).

———. "Metaphysical Enquiry." *Theoria to Theory* 12 (1978).

———. "The Privacy of Experience." *Mind* 77 (1969).

———. *Santayana: An Examination of His Philosophy*. London: Routledge & Kegan Paul, 1974.

———. *The Vindication of Absolute Idealism*. Edinburgh: Edinburgh University Press, 1983.

Strawson, P. F. *Individuals: An Essay in Descriptive Metaphysics*. London: Methuen & Co., 1964.

Taylor, A. E. *The Elements of Metaphysics*. London: Methuen & Co., 1961.

———. "F. H. Bradley." *Mind* 34 (1925).

———. "F. H. Bradley." *Proceedings of the British Academy* 21 (1924–25).

Vlastos, G. "Organic Categories in Whitehead." *Journal of Philosophy* 34 (1937).

Waddington, C. H. *Beyond Appearance.* Edinburgh: Edinburgh University Press, 1969.

———. *Evolution of an Evolutionist.* Edinburgh: Edinburgh University Press, 1974.

———. ed. *Towards a Theoretical Biology.* Vols. 1 and 2. Edinburgh: Edinburgh University Press, 1968.

Weisenbeck, J. D. *Alfred North Whitehead's Philosophy of Value.* Waukesha: Thomas Press, 1969.

Whitehead, A. N. *Adventures of Ideas.* New York: The Free Press, 1961.

———. *Concept of Nature.* Cambridge: Cambridge University Press, 1926.

———. *An Enquiry Concerning the Principles of Natural Knowledge.* Cambridge: Cambridge University Press, 1925.

———. *Essays in Science and Philosophy.* London: Rider and Co., 1948.

———. *The Function of Reason.* Boston: The Beacon Press, 1958.

———. *Interpretation of Science,* ed. A. H. Johnson. Indianapolis: Bobbs-Merrill Co., 1961.

———. *Modes of Thought.* New York: Capricorn Books, 1958.

———. *Principia Mathematica,* with Bertrand Russell. Vols. 1–3. Cambridge: Cambridge University Press, 2nd ed. 1927.

———. *The Principle of Relativity.* Cambridge: Cambridge University Press, 1922.

———. *Process and Reality,* corrected edition, eds. D. R. Griffin and D. W. Sherburne. New York: The Free Press, 1978.

———. *Religion in the Making.* Cambridge: Cambridge University Press, 1930.

————. *Symbolism: Its Meaning and Effect*. New York: Macmillan and Co., 1927.

————. *Science and the Modern World*. New York: The Free Press, 1967.

Whittemore, R. C. "The Metaphysics of Whitehead's Feeling." *Tulane Studies in Philosophy* 10 (1961).

————. "Time and Whitehead's God." *Tulane Studies in Philosophy* 4 (1955).

————. "Whitehead's Process and Bradley's Reality." *The Modern Schoolman* 32 (1954–55).

Wolf, George. "Psychological Physiology from the Standpoint of a Physiological Psychologist." *Process Studies* 11 (1981).

Wollheim, Richard. *F. H. Bradley*. Middlesex: Penguin Books, 1969.

INDEX